Julius Caesar
and Me

FRONTISPIECE: *Photograph from 2012 RSC production of* Julius Caesar *with Paterson Joseph as Brutus and Cyril Nri as Cassius. (Credit: Photograph by Kwame Lestrade © RSC)*

Julius Caesar and Me

Exploring Shakespeare's African Play

Paterson Joseph

methuen | drama

LONDON · NEW YORK · OXFORD · NEW DELHI · SYDNEY

METHUEN DRAMA
Bloomsbury Publishing Plc
50 Bedford Square, London, WC1B 3DP, UK

BLOOMSBURY, METHUEN DRAMA and the Methuen Drama logo are trademarks of
Bloomsbury Publishing Plc

First published in Great Britain 2018

Cover design: Eleanor Rose
Cover photograph by Kwame Lestrade

A catalogue record for this book is available from the British Library.

A catalog record for this book is available from the Library of Congress.

ISBN:	HB:	978-1-3500-1122-9
	PB:	978-1-3500-1118-2
	ePDF:	978-1-3500-1119-9
	eBook:	978-1-3500-1120-5

Series: Theatre Makers

Typeset by RefineCatch Limited, Bungay, Suffolk
Printed and bound in Great Britain

To find out more about our authors and books visit www.bloomsbury.com and sign up for
our newsletters.

For the son of my dreams – Cj. x

CONTENTS

LIST OF ILLUSTRATIONS

FOREWORD

How many ages hence
Shall this our lofty scene be acted o'er
In states unborn and accents yet unknown

(*JC* 3.1.111–13)

Shakespeare's *Julius Caesar* has always spoken to the moment. As I write this, controversy rages in New York where a production of the play in Central Park casts Caesar as Donald Trump, complete with orange comb-over, which has so outraged the right-wing press that nervous sponsors have withdrawn their support.

In 2012, I directed a production of the play at Stratford-upon-Avon for the Royal Shakespeare Company (RSC). It was filmed for the British Broadcasting Corporation (BBC), transferred to the West End, and subsequently invited to New York, and Moscow.

Paterson Joseph played Brutus. The success of the production was due in no small measure to his performance.

Paterson is undoubtedly one of the best actors of his generation. The fact that he may be unknown to some, is no doubt because the opportunities available to others were not as available to him. And yet, Paterson is a pioneer, forging a path where others have followed. Hailed by Nicholas Hytner, ex-artistic director of the National Theatre, as 'a classical actor of massive presence', Paterson makes his craft seem effortless. His art is to hide his technique, but that technique is forged by dedication and long commitment to his craft, as a superlative classical actor. He now appears before us as a writer, a serious chronicler of his art.

Julius Caesar dissects the ruthless politics of power. Brutus can be seen as both a republican hero or a wishy-washy liberal who doesn't see things through. Is he a bullying dogmatist, or a romantic idealist? Either way, his actions create a vacuum into which much more ruthless people will run. In assassinating Caesar, Brutus and Cassius bring about precisely the opposite of what they seek to achieve, and usher in the downfall of the Republic.

Ultimately Brutus is both idealist and vain egotist and Paterson caught that ambivalence perfectly, in a brilliant performance.

My acquaintance with *Julius Caesar* goes back particularly to 1987, when I first joined the RSC as an actor and played Octavius Caesar under

Terry Hands' direction. Watching many productions of the play over the years has alerted me to an essential conundrum: that its urgent resonance in the modern world is somehow harder to achieve if the play is set in togas and sandals, and yet if it is set in a contemporary Western context, too often the play's almost mythic reverberation gets lost, and the assassination seems merely like the elimination of a particularly belligerent chairman of the board.

It was not until I directed *Titus Andronicus* at the Market Theatre in Johannesburg, at the end of the apartheid era, that I began to see how Shakespeare's plays could somehow resonate more precisely and urgently in an African context. As the South African writer Can Themba suggested, 'the turbulence of urban African life is like the stage of Shakespeare's Elizabethan world ... Shakespeare reaches out a fraternal hand to the throbbing heart of Africa'.

In *Julius Caesar*, the references to soothsayers, ancestor spirits, and lions stalking the streets are suddenly entirely congruent in an African setting. But the fierce frequency with which the Continent has witnessed freedom fighters rising to power on a wave of popularity, only to concentrate that power into a corrupt ruling elite, gave the play a new immediacy. It seemed to provide a potent context for what the great South African actor John Kani called simply 'Shakespeare's African play'. A noble and notable exception to these liberator-dictators was, of course, Nelson Mandela, who autographed lines from *Julius Caesar* in a copy of the complete works smuggled into the prison on Robben Island: a perhaps surprising endorsement which Paterson describes in these pages, and which ultimately was the ignition for our whole production.

Paterson Joseph declares that this production of *Julius Caesar* was 'the most affecting production' he has ever worked on. In his intense and vivid account of how it came about, and the journey it took, he is nevertheless openly honest about the ups and downs of what became quite a rollercoaster ride.

It is a heartfelt, funny and sometimes startling account of a production which I think, for both of us, was a life, and a career-changing event.

Gregory Doran
Artistic Director
Royal Shakespeare Company
Stratford-upon-Avon
June 2017

PREFACE

I started to write this account as a method of debriefing from my experiences working on William Shakespeare's *Julius Caesar* for the Royal Shakespeare Company, between July 2011 and April 2013. I got far more out of putting pen to paper than I bargained for.

While it felt important to note the events and some of the feelings they elicited in me, it became increasingly obvious that I needed more than just a cursory reporting of this time. It expanded to include a large chunk of autobiography in order to contextualize my attitudes and my unique perspective. The first third of the book is about how I came to be standing on any stage, anywhere, given where I started.

Theatrical accounts are not, naturally, interesting to all of us. I hope, however, even if you don't really burn for the subject matter, you can still take some pleasure from being given a window into the workings of another world. I may have over-explained some things on the one hand and neglected to clarify some theatre jargon on the other. Apologies for that. No apologies, though, for the truth I express of how I felt both positively and negatively, during this marathon run.

It is, then, a very personal, I hope informative, view of tackling one monumental play from the thirty-seven strong Shakespeare canon. It is not a book that mirrors any academic textbook on *Julius Caesar*. There are plenty of those. Rather, I am on the inside, trying to make sense of a story that was as new to me as it will be to a young student, taking it on for the first time. As unfamiliar to me as to a reluctant theatre-goer, scared that they just won't *get it*. This unique perspective should help alleviate any feelings of apprehension that might be elicited from an overtly scholarly take on the play.

As a student, I would have loved to have read an actor's account that spoke to me in language I could understand, of the wonder of the work of this remarkable Warwickshire man. An account that would teach and entertain while debunking the myth of Shakespeare, yet leaving me still in awe of his wonderful and uncanny plays, sonnets and songs. This work is an attempt to help fill that gap on the Theatre Studies shelf.

My experiences from a working-class, Afro-Caribbean origin, to becoming a leading actor at that most Establishment of establishments, the Royal Shakespeare Company, will be an eye-opener for many. The challenges that actors who are not white face just entering into this arena are many and labyrinthine. Add to this the fact that we had three actors in our company who were black women and one can see how rich this viewpoint may prove to be.

My fellow performers, Adjoa Andoh, Samantha Lawson and Ann Ogbomo all faced challenges living with a company of men for more than a year, as we worked on this most masculine of plays. I would suggest their perspectives on this may show that – even when an acting company comprises fifteen men and only three women, in a play that deals mainly with male struggles for dominance – this can, perhaps surprisingly, leave room for the strong, female voice in a world of testosterone and violence. Shakespeare recognized this potential gender dynamic better than any of his contemporaries. (By the way, I will adopt the prevailing address of both male and female performers as *actors* rather than *actor/actress*.)

Audience reactions will also be tackled. This is, after all, the coal-face of our particular art. I will relate the conversations I have had with psychologists and neurologists on the subject of what exactly it is that happens between performer and spectator. I will delve into the murky area of de-role-ing, where an actor fights to shed the skin of his character; sometimes with success but, occasionally, with a degree of damage. How we as individuals negotiate this transformation into and out of character, forms an interesting backdrop to the work on the stage.

Warning: All of the descriptions of the events in this journey are from my own perspective. Where possible, I have tried to give the viewpoint of most of the protagonists, but that has not always been feasible. I can only say in my defence, that I am aware of being subjective in all my comments. I am not so deluded as to suppose them a definitive rendering of actual events. I had some wonderful times and some tough times, too. This book reflects the light, as well as the dark, moments of a journey I found fascinating.

My too grand hope? That one day *Julius Caesar and Me* will be a regular and trusted resource for students and teachers, alike. Affording an autobiographical view on an actor's origin and art; a new angle on a text that appears so often on the school syllabus; and, optimistically, an intriguing and accessible entry into the works of our greatest British export: William Shakespeare.

Paterson Joseph
London, May 2017

ACKNOWLEDGEMENTS

The worst part of a book for any writer. The moment when we realize that there are way too many people to thank for the creation of a piece. It should rightly be called **Apologies.** *Of course, I hope – having said all this – to have covered my forgetful back.*

I'd like to thank the following:

Lucy Fawcett, Gaia Banks and all the staff at Sheil Land Associates, my literary agents who were the first to imagine this might actually *be* a book. Anna Brewer and all at Methuen Drama who took on this fledgling author at his most vulnerable and taught him how to write in comprehensible sentences. My particular thanks to my editors there: Camilla Erskine and Lucy Brown. Confidence-builders Alexander Cooke, Louise Donald, India Sinclair and all the smart cats at Hamilton Hodell, my agents.

Gregory Doran for his brave kindness in allowing me to quote from his private correspondence with a struggling actor and an even braver early reader. Cyril Nri, for his generosity of spirit. A true friend, collaborator and brother for life.

My parents Antony and Amelia Joseph for never standing in the way of my acting career. Emmanuelle Joseph, for single-handedly holding the family fort during the long run of *Caesar*. The late Richard Laws and his wife Pamela; the first friends to gently insist I write my experiences down. Two of the world's great listeners.

My friend and first reader, Marion Molteno, author extraordinaire. Your notes made all the difference. Sara Belle, Jane Hudson, Jami Rogers and Tilusha Ghelani who read or listened to me read sections of the book before it was quite ready for public consumption. Indulgence beyond the call of friendship!

Gretchen Gerzina, author and historian, whose works inspire me. I thank you.

Finally, to the outlandishly talented cast and crew of *Julius Caesar*, and all at the RSC, without whom none of this would have been possible or half so much fun.

To you all, my heartfelt gratitude and deep respect.

Paterson Joseph
10 August 2017

Prologue:

The Marvel of Shakespeare

I'm five years old. Playing *cars* on the floor of the living room at home. We lived above a bric-a-brac shop called *This 'n' That* on Willesden High Road, north-west London. It's 1969.

My dad's tall, thin, Jamaican friend Lloyd has just arrived. He looks down at me. Asks, in his drawling, Jamaican accent, what he always asks me whenever he sees me:

'Whappum, Doc?'

So much cooler than Bugs Bunny's version, I thought. And Lloyd pronounced it, 'Dark'.

Dad and Lloyd then got down to their usual business of swapping Marvel and DC comics. Lloyd's favourite by a long way was *Thor – God of Thunder*. I had read the *Thor* comics with much less interest and comprehension than I had the *Spiderman* comics which my dad favoured as, of course, did I.

Always found those ones harder to read than Spidey, Iron Man, Superman, etc. Why was the language so weird? But just then, Lloyd pipes up:

'You know, *T'or* is just like de Bible! Thee and Thy and t'ing?'

'Eehee!' says Dad in assent. Dad then, memorably, added this:

'Bible, yes, but more like a kinda . . . ***Shakespeare*** . . .'

He paused, I seem to remember, as he watched the slowly dawning bliss of recognition on Lloyd's face. Who simply said:

'Yea, maaan . . .!'

In the awed silence at their own brilliance that followed, I looked at both my heroes and thought:

'I have *got* to find out how this *Shakespeare* could delight Tony and Lloyd more than even *Marvel Comics*!'

And later, much later, I did.

1

First Words . . .

Words have long been a big part of my life, ever since the day my mother sat us all down and decided that, instead of their native St Lucian Kweol, we would only speak English in the house. She and my father had come from St Lucia in the Caribbean in the late 1950s. My mother Amelia once said that she'd heard about my dad Tony and his wild ways, before she left the island. They actually met in London, shortly after they both arrived from the Caribbean. Part of that great exodus beginning in 1948 with the docking of the MV *Empire Windrush*, at Tilbury in London. Though it is a tiny island, they grew up on very different sides of the tracks. Mum was a singleton with a mother who was, to all intents and purposes, a single mum. Not a phrase that would have been current then, of course. But it described the life of an absent father precisely. My gran would sell her baked goods from island to island, leaving mum in the care of her four aunts. A quiet, obedient and refined girl. Dad, on the other hand, had come up the hard way; his parents parcelling the boisterous child out to strict godparents in the country. He grew up with a hell of a lot more freedom than my mum, however. And he loved a party. In many ways, they were totally incompatible. The quiet, religious girl and the roustabout, Brylcreemed, man-about-town. A minor miracle, then, that they stayed together until I was eighteen.

They married in 1958, having five kids by 1964. Frank, Glenda, Jacqueline, Pamela then me. Bella, my younger sister, came along some years later. Both my parents worked low paid jobs in factories. Mum also did piece-work at home, sewing sleeves and scarves for a few shillings an item. We didn't have much money to spare. We never starved – though, as growing kids, we were frequently hungry. We lived very frugally, but were always immaculately turned out by our mum; scrimping and saving for school uniforms, making garments for my sisters, grooming their hair to perfection. Not without tears, alas, poor girls. She worked particularly hard on our manners. We were always polite and were taught to respect our elders. And the one area we were never allowed to cut loose in was our language. No swearing. No bad grammar. No backchat.

As an immigrant, your radar is very sharply attuned. You listen for language signals in a heightened way. How else can you keep yourself safe in a potentially hostile environment, if you aren't aware of the meanings and interpretations of words? It is the immigrant's best armour. Anyone not able to master the language and customs quickly, will soon find themselves struggling to get work, promotion, even decent housing. One's ability to negotiate the official ropes dictates one's success or failure in the system. It's a tough place to start one's life but an ideal training ground for the harsh realities of the world.

Mum's survival strategy was to ensure we did not have St Lucian accents when speaking English. That disadvantage, she considered, could be easily remedied. And it happened one day when I was just three. She informed us that she and my father would only speak English to us from that day onwards. I was only told when I was in my thirties that this had occurred; I had no recollection of the moment. Yet, strange to say, actual memories of those times have always haunted me. Real incidences, that would come back again and again. Like a trauma regularly revisited. These persistent memories are now explained by my mother's decision on that significant day. The first memory is being about four years old. I was chasing my mum around the flat one morning. Everyone had gone to school and I wasn't due to start till the following autumn. As I followed my harassed mum around, I asked her incessant questions about the objects in the room:

'Mummy, how do you say "scissors", in patois?' 'Mummy, how do you say, "television"?' She was truly nettled at these questions for reasons I couldn't possibly have fathomed at that young age. Kept on telling me not to ask her, anymore. It was odd for me. 'Mummy, how do you say "fridge" in patois?' 'How do you say "sausages"?' The more I asked, the more annoyed she got. Finally, she snapped at me. Told me to stop asking. And I did. I didn't ever bother her again about it. Even as young as four, I could sense it was a sore point. I simply didn't want to annoy her. She had so many things that seemed to irritate her and this was only one of many nuisances she could do without. Though my questions stopped, I still, naturally, maintained my desire to know the names for things. It was as if my whole world was replaced overnight with one where the language of that world was very different from before. And the naming of objects is such a vital part of the human story; our way of making sense of a frighteningly unpredictable world. I sometimes wonder if our parents regretted cutting us off from the language of their culture so violently. Back in 1967, however, they must have felt compelled to do this. I know that today, whenever I visit St Lucia, I am frequently disappointed at my inability to communicate with the locals in their own language.

My second memory comes from infant school. In class, at the age of six, I was asked by the teacher to tell everyone what I had had for Sunday lunch. My answer: 'Chicken with rice and peas', was met with gales of laughter from my classmates. They were mostly kids born in Ireland or with Eire-born parents who had only just arrived in the UK. I suppose that would excuse their ignorance of Caribbean cuisine. I continued, 'And salad, with tomato, lettuce and coocoomba . . .' The silence was heavy for a second.

Then, quick as a whip, I said, 'Cucumber'. I tried to never make an error like that again. It was a moment that had a major and lasting impact on my life. I felt then that I must not open my mouth publicly without thinking. I became quite taciturn, only speaking freely in the playground with my few friends or with my siblings and relatives at home. This caution stayed with me for decades.

I was like the proverbial sponge when it came to language. I read anything that came my way. Thanks to my older sisters playing *school* with me, I could read well by the time I was four. I also loved to listen to BBC Radio 1 or Radio 2. The voices were soothing and colloquial. I'm convinced I learnt to speak a kind of *clean* version of English from listening daily to these broadcasts. I would also imitate newscasters and chat show hosts when I watched TV. Even the driest political debates would be ideal fodder for my language games. I'd repeat everything that was said, even acting out the speaker's facial expressions and serious manner. I may have begun to replace any *natural* speech patterns with the ones I was hearing in the media around me at this time. Isn't imitation the sincerest form of flattery? I wanted so much to be and sound as smart as those people on the telly or on the radio.

* * *

My favourite primary school teacher, Mrs Claudette 'Birdie' Bird, should be credited with being the first person to introduce me to the world of William Shakespeare, via Charles and Mary Lamb's *Tales from Shakespeare*. A book written in 1807 whose aim was to introduce Shakespeare's themes to children. For all her affection for me, I was far from Mrs Bird's star pupil when it came to academia. I think I was a bit of a mystery to her, too. I was a good public reader and was clearly smart, at least with my sharp tongue. However, when it came to my school work . . .? I did make her laugh, though, and she has stuck with me to this day. Perhaps the isolation of being the only black child in infant school, along with my language challenges, caused me to be rather withdrawn throughout my academic life. I was ignored for the most part or told point blank that I was 'too bold' or just plain 'thick'. So, apart from the odd smart-arsed comment, I kept quiet in class, saving all my energies and focus for the playground.

But there were pockets of light relief in these early academic years. My first acting assignment was as 'Cow' in the First Year's nativity play. People found my 'Cow' voice – all slow, low and chewy – funny. I didn't altogether understand why, really. What else could I have done? I was a cow! My most memorable primary school acting experience was in the musical *Oliver!* I was cast as the villainous Bill Sykes. In retrospect, I'd guess that the casting was suspiciously stereotypical but at the time I simply thought it was a great part. Thankfully, that sort of race-biased thinking hadn't infected my young psyche, quite yet.

Oliver! came as I was about to leave the relatively safe haven of Mary Magdalene's Roman Catholic Primary School (Mixed) in Willesden, for the terror of Cardinal Hinsley Secondary School (Boys) in Harlesden, north-west London; with its aggressive older boys, race fights and lack of females. My brother Franklin – the eldest sibling – and I may have shared a room, but I was very close to my three older sisters. Bella, ten years younger than me, was in my charge for most of her formative years, giving me the chance to be the older brother; a role I relished. At the tender age of ten and a half, therefore, Cardinal Hinsley seemed very male and very alien compared to the world I had grown up in. Ours was, in the final analysis, a very female household despite my dad's sometimes unnecessarily disciplinarian outbursts. Mum was a strong force without violence; a little uncommon amongst my Afro-Caribbean contemporaries. No judgement here. Our parents came from tough childhoods where discipline was swift and draconian. Whips, belts, switches, slippers, canes and worst of all, hands. It was like a medal of honour ceremony to hear us kids telling our tales of 'catching licks', laughing all the while.

I don't remember very much of the *Oliver!* rehearsal process, though I can remember being as happy and engaged as I had ever been in all my difficult school years.

I recall something our director – a rare male teacher – said: 'You are the only person playing your part in the whole world. No one else. Be excited. And know that you're special.' I wish every director would start the rehearsal process like that on day one.

The joyful rehearsals wiped out sour memories, too. I had just flunked the dreaded eleven-plus. Had no clue how to answer some questions. Was defeated even before I began to open the folded-over, double-sided, exam paper. I merely answered questions with random answers. Unless it was about words – the sections that asked about stories or ideas were my only solace in those lost two hours or so. I remember feeling a sense of uselessness, knowing I had, bar a million-to-one cosmic glitch, answered all the maths questions with random, certainly wrong, answers. What was I thinking of? Nothing. I had no proper context for these tests. I couldn't have known they would determine my academic future and beyond. How could I? And, indeed, how could they tell us? Cruel enough to decide a child's fate at the age of seven then eleven. Worse still, if the creature knows it's being done.

Opening night of *Oliver!* came and the buzz was powerful. I recall a powerful sense of focus, of trying to stay calm. When I made my entrance into the packed assembly hall, I had an immediate feeling I'd entered a private space; tangibly different from the one outside. This space and the audience seated in it seemed to hold its breath. Collectively. Waiting for signals, some physical, some verbal, to let them know what to think. I became instantly aware that my every move meant something, so grew very still and attentive. At the time, of course, I only took all this in instinctively and wouldn't have been capable of articulating my impressions. My first line after my scene with Fagin, when the audience first see the villain I am, elicited a roar of laughter I'll never forget as long as I live. Spontaneous, warm and full of a fierce affection. Applause rang in my ears. I had never felt so loved, and by so many. Delicious. Probably, addictive. I could almost feel my natural shyness evaporating onstage.

As Glenda, my eldest sister, walked me home to the flat, we met the mother of one of my best friends. She regaled Glenda with detailed descriptions of my performance, my talent, my fans. Glenda, bemused, impressed, thanked her and promised to tell mum. I was full of a kind of inner satisfaction. A new sensation for me. I'd been noticed. We walked on, as I gazed at the moon peeking through one of those frequent 1970s London fogs. I felt that I had found the only thing that had ever thrilled me. And that thing, this acting, had also thrilled others. Even at ten, I suspected that there would not be an infinite number of moments like this in my life.

* * *

My first, visceral, encounter with Shakespeare's plays came when I was about fourteen, at a time when I was buried under layers of shyness as self-protection. Circa 1978. My best mate Tony Leonce had decided that he wanted to try acting when the careers options came up. I admired Tony. I dreamt I could be confident like him. Hairy, like him: he could grow a beard! I imagined in time I would be tall and quick-witted and good at comedy like him. Tony's answer to the whole enterprise of careers advice was to shop around. That should have alerted me to the fact that he wasn't altogether committed to his expressed goal of being an actor. The guy was my best mate, though, so I said I'd audition with him for the National Youth Theatre (NYT). An organization whose existence was known to me about a hot two minutes before I signed up to audition with my talented pal. Couple of days later he had pulled out, choosing a career in catering, instead. To my horror, I realized that I was already booked to audition for a place at this prestigious theatre company.

The NYT has been the nursery of young, British acting talent for over sixty years and is widely believed to be the first dedicated youth theatre company in the world. Daniel Day Lewis, Andrea Riseborough, Adrian Lester, Kate Winslet, Ralph Fiennes, Zawe Ashton, David Harewood and Gugu Mbatha-Raw are just a few of its more recent, illustrious alumni. Nothing about this celebrated theatre company was known to me at the time, of course.

I asked my history teacher who also taught drama if she could guide me through my audition. I hadn't thought to choose Theatre Studies as an option. Not sure why. I suppose it felt like a soft subject to choose in a school run on muscle and sport. Art, music and dance were for girls. Children. Pansies. We were men and we did manly things. A tedious attitude it would have been great to have pushed against. But, busy parents and an uninformed kid are not a good combination for finding a route into the performance arts. Not then and especially not now. So much of our arts for schools and Theatre in Education (TIE) budgets have been slashed or have disappeared entirely. Confidence grows from performing. As a shy teen, mine would certainly have been greatly improved by an outlet like a drama group. And educationalists tell me that confidence in oneself is the first step to achieving academic excellence.

The history teacher handed me a book of audition speeches for boys. She chose a monologue from an obscure Michael Redgrave play about Roundheads and Cavaliers. No clue why she thought that would be a good fit for me. It wasn't memorable and it wasn't my favourite of the three pieces I had been asked to prepare. The second was much more up my street: *Jabberwocky*, by Lewis Carroll. I loved it from the moment I read the first lines:

> 'Twas brillig, and the slithy toves
> Did gyre and gimble in the wabe:
> All mimsy were the borogoves,
> And the mome raths outgrabe.

I revelled in this new language; these made-up words. Loved the way they felt when they formed in my mouth. It was like waking up a part of my imagination that teenage-hood, shyness, had all but obscured. The part of me that liked to perform. To entertain. Though it wasn't really as straightforward as that. It wasn't attention per se that I was after. In fact, I liked the shadows. I had become habituated to the low expectations people had of me. I think performing was more about affirming my existence: I am here. You can see me. Therefore, I matter.

I acted out *Jabberwocky* to illustrate the story. Not entirely sure if it was any good. I did get really into it, I recall. I could see the scary beasts as described by the old father:

> 'Beware the Jabberwock, my son!
> The jaws that bite, the claws that catch!
> Beware the Jubjub bird, and shun
> The frumious Bandersnatch!'

I remember the delight I took in putting on the old man's voice I'd created for the bit that goes:

> 'And hast thou slain the Jabberwock?
> Come to my arms, my beamish boy!
> O frabjous day! Callooh! Callay!'
> He chortled in his joy.

The last piece had to be a Shakespeare soliloquy. I was learning so many new words, already. Monologue. Soliloquy. Audition. The history teacher simply handed me a book and I was told to find and learn a three-minute speech from it. No questions, no discussions, no help. I was going to do a speech from *The Merchant of Venice* whether I wanted to or not. *The Merchant of Venice*. A story that was as unfamiliar to me as the plot for, say, *Cymbeline* is unfamiliar to all but the most ardent Shakespearean. What was *The Merchant of Venice*? What happens in it? A persecuted, money-lending Jew? A blood bond? An anti-Semitic, Christian community? A cross-dressing, Venetian defence lawyer? None of these things were familiar to me. This auditioning enterprise was feeling less like a doss – a way to skip lessons legitimately – and more like a chore.

I took the book home somewhat despondently. I loved reading, ordinarily. I had done even before starting infant school. My sisters had used me not just in their plays and performances for our parents but also as a guinea pig pupil for all their games of *school*. Then from thirteen years old, after reading the astounding C. S. Lewis novel *The Lion, the Witch and the Wardrobe,* I became book obsessed. The written word seemed extraordinary to me suddenly. Black squiggles on a page became the magical land of Narnia; a wardrobe of fur coats; the castle at Cair Paravel and the White Queen, and not forgetting the kindly and heroic Mr Tumnus. Willesden Green faded away the moment I opened that book back then. I didn't read in any systematic way. I'd go from reading Oscar Wilde, to English translations of Guy de Maupassant's short stories, then on to sister Pam's Mills and Boon romances, by way of Enid Blyton with a smattering of salacious Harold Robbins thrown in. All of these books were sourced randomly from various family members. I couldn't get enough of them. I'd been sneaking out to the library – instead of going to school – ever since the idea occurred to me when I was about thirteen. I kept this up until I left school at fifteen years old. Whilst I regret dearly my wholesale rejection of the school system, I maintain that I will have learnt more from my jaunts to the library than I would ever have learnt from the strange, bullying, neglectful system they had at Cardinal Hinsley.

Now, here I was with a book that might have seemed daunting in school. But I wasn't at school. I could read it aloud, in a loud voice if I wanted. And that is precisely what I did. I sight-read Shakespeare, having never heard or read any plays, apart from *Oliver!,* before. Speaking all the parts just as I thought they might sound.

The most important thing about that moment was not the sounds I was making, exactly. More the fact that I was making sounds. I was speaking, confidently. Sounding smart too, because I was using words my contemporaries were totally unfamiliar with, frankly. Not only that, I got it. I actually understood the story and felt the sympathy one needs to, in order that Shylock not be a stock stage-villain. Like a punch to the solar plexus, it struck me then that Shakespeare wasn't at all mysterious or incomprehensible to the likes of me. If *I* could get it with no instructions to speak of, then anybody could. It might be easy to underestimate the impact of this moment and I might not have remembered it so clearly if I hadn't been in the position of having to learn part of this text. But if the truth is that a poorly-educated, son of an immigrant can grasp the themes, emotions and intellectual power of Shakespeare with little or no previous experience of him, then he is truly a universal playwright. I felt an ownership of Shakespeare that day and that confidence that he belongs to me, too, has never left me.

* * *

I'm getting off the number 18 double-decker bus from Harlesden and walking to the Shaw Theatre in Marylebone to audition for the NYT. It has always been difficult for me to recollect many details of the day. I suspect the terror of what I was attempting took over my rational brain. I recall vague snapshots – fragments of the day. Walking to the theatre; feeling the terror as of a condemned man; nervously waiting in a small room; starting my Roundheads and Cavaliers piece; a white man of about thirty, watching me from a desk down one end of the room. The *Jabberwocky* piece is a blank. Then came the Shylock and I only remember shyly – purposefully – turning away from the man watching me as I focused on addressing my imaginary, Christian enemy, Antonio:

> Signor Antonio, many a time and oft
> In the Rialto you have rated me
> About my moneys and my usances . . .

(MV 1.3.102–4)

The next thing I know, I'm sitting opposite this man and he's asking me why I want to join the NYT. I looked down to my right for ages, struggling to think of the appropriate answer. The silence was interminable and, still looking down, I finally squeezed out sincerely – but painfully quietly – 'Because I like meeting people.' Poor, shy kid, he must have thought. And then probably, 'He'll never fit in here.' The letter arrived very shortly afterwards to let me know that I had been unsuccessful. When I think of this now and with what I know about the difficulties that young, urban kids have with looking authority figures in the eye, I can see from his perspective how this might have seemed a no-brainer failure. To him, a well-educated, probably middle-class, white man, my behaviour might even have come across as unconvincing, unfathomable. The cultural and class divide at the NYT has narrowed somewhat today and, as a current student mentor, I have seen that they have made great strides in diversifying the pool of actors they take on. Back then, however, my shyness would have been interpreted as something insurmountable, incompatible even, with the culture of the NYT and British theatre culture in general.

Although my timidity (and perhaps my performance) meant that I was not successful in my audition for the NYT, the whole process of reading plays, learning lines and rehearsing by myself was a catalyst for awakening in me a sense of self-worth and intelligence. It should rightly be recognized then, as the beginnings of an outrageous idea: That I might just have a brain and a talent hidden, somewhere, deep down.

2

. . . Words . . . Words . . .

The Royal Free Hospital in London's Hampstead Heath has been my workplace for several months. I'm seventeen. Mum works upstairs as a ward orderly. I'm in the basement kitchen, desperate to learn how to be a chef. After six months, they promised to send me to college to study for the highest catering qualification available; a City and Guilds 706 (1) and (2). If I could get that, the world would, surely, be my oyster. Chefs can work anywhere, my best friend Tony Leonce had told me; and the City and Guilds diplomas were recognized around the globe. Dad's sister, my Auntie Helena, had lived in Toronto for many years. My present goal was to get out of England and seek my fortune there. I just needed that diploma. But here I was, nine months later, being told I would have to wait till the following September to start my course. More ham and cheese sandwiches made by the hundreds, more boiled eggs to be shelled, rinsed and sliced for hundreds of salads and sarnies. Stirring that huge vat of porridge every morning was a strangely unappetizing start to my day; only slicing the wooden oar through a massive cauldron of minced lamb for shepherd's pie was worse. Despite all this, I tried to hold firm to my goal of becoming a chef until, finally, my patience with the Royal Free ran out on one memorable day.

The whole of the catering staff had been asked to clean behind the unused food-trolleys at the back of the kitchens. There were about thirty of these huge, tray-stacking trolleys. The area had not been cleaned for some time, certainly never in the months that I had worked there. So the clean-up was long overdue. As we began to move the trolleys aside, it instantly became apparent that the odd bug that had visited the kitchen had not been alone. A writhing, black sea of cockroaches greeted us when we finally rolled these metal containers aside. It seemed as if the whole floor area was undulating, as their bodies crawled over each other, desperate to escape the bleach, boots and brooms that had come to wreak utter destruction on their close-knit community. Maybe it was an unreasonably disproportionate response to this stomach-churning incident but I knew from that moment that catering wasn't for me long term. Perhaps not coincidentally, the longing to do something creative as a career had returned to me at that time.

Fortunately, I was a bit of a paper hoarder and rarely threw anything away. One of my treasures was a large envelope where I kept my NYT rejection letter and a few other leaflets for youth theatres and drama clubs. I suppose my history teacher had given them to me as a salve after my failure to get in to the NYT. As I sat reading the rejection letter, noting the NYT logo with envy, I remember thinking: 'I know I was rejected, but shouldn't I have one more go? At least when I talk to my grandchildren I can tell them I tried.' Not exactly Henry V's 'Once more unto the breach, dear friends'. But pretty rousing for a shy, insecure seventeen-year-old. And so, that evening, I telephoned one of the theatres I had found amongst the leaflets in my special envelope. It was called The Cockpit and was in Marylebone, west London; not very far from where I lived. I very formally said, in my politest voice, 'Hello. May I come and audition to be part of your youth theatre, please?' There was a longish pause and I suspect now, a suppressed giggle, as the lady on the other end said, smilingly, 'No, you don't need to audition here, dear. It's free and it's open to all.' Blimey. Talk about a warm welcome. And such a sharp contrast to the harsher voices of authority that I had been used to all my life. These guys sounded cool.

The night I arrived at the Cockpit changed my life. No exaggeration here. Instant and permanent change. I had taken up a position in the theatre bar/foyer, where I could do what I had learnt to do in large groups: take stock of everything and everyone. That strategy helped to obviate the fear that I might say or do something inappropriate. A real child-of-an-immigrant pattern of thinking, this. 'Don't stand out. Don't say the wrong thing.' I saw how confident all these kids were. They faced each other, were tactile, loud, free and confident. I would love to be like that, I thought.

We gathered in the rehearsal room upstairs to play games that were designed to break the ice and warm us up. They did the trick, as I felt much freer after half an hour of fooling about. Later, we were asked to form small groups of two or three in order to improvise sketches. I had never heard the word improvise before, to my knowledge. Certainly, I didn't know what it meant in this context. Thankfully, my fellow performer was au fait with all the jargon, so he instructed me in great detail about the precise meaning of the word. 'Improvisation: Erm . . . it means we just make stuff up?' OK, I thought, that's easy. I don't recall who suggested it, but we chose to pretend to be two guys working on a building site. Don't remember being nervous at all. I think I was having so much fun laughing at everyone else's improvs that, by the time it came around the room to us, I had been too distracted to think much about what we would actually do.

We stood in the middle of the room with all eyes on us. I channelled a memory of working with my dad and his fellow labourers – he had recently trained to be a plasterer – and began miming placing a brick on the low wall we were suddenly building. Without much consultation, my acting partner and I just got into it. A gently audible intake of breath signalled that the other actors recognized what we were doing. They laughed. They got it. And here was the miracle that kept me doing what I do for the next thirty-five years. We didn't have actual bricks in our hands. We were not building a visible wall. We were pretending to be people we were not. And yet, the spectators had bought into our made-up world. They had imbued what we had merely imagined with solidity, humanity and humour.

This was the performance equivalent of my excitement as I started reading *The Lion, the Witch and the Wardrobe*, when I was thirteen – only much more addictive. This magical transaction between audience and performer was astounding to me and unexpectedly life-affirming. We could collaborate on a creative idea and together bring it to life, first in me and then in them. A revolution in my thinking and being. A sea-change, that led me to leave the Royal Free Hospital almost overnight and head to drama school.

It's worth noting here that, as a young actor, I received great encouragement at the Cockpit. It was a space designed for the largely working-class, Lisson Grove community and, every summer, a play was performed by a group of youths sourced locally, as well as from the wider London area. We were all aged between sixteen and twenty-four. Invaluable cultural exchanges happen in places like the Cockpit and this first encounter with middle-class kids gave me the confidence to know that they were just like me. I was blown away by the talent and self-assurance of all these young people. Acting is, undoubtedly, the source of my ability to express myself in any environment now. It was not a likely prospect if you could have seen me as the shy mumbler of seventeen.

A TIE director at the Cockpit once overheard me commenting on being a black person in the acting profession. Comments parroted from my sister Pam, who feared I was only destined for menial roles. He urged me to think about the other students taking part in our youth theatre programme. He pointed out that some of them would go on to be writers. These writers would, inevitably, write about what they know. And what do they see around them? A multi-cultural, multi-ethnic world. This, he predicted, would be the shape and look of British theatre, television and film to come. Quite a vision and one that I believed then would soon come to pass.

* * *

I randomly chose Studio '68 of Theatre Arts from the pages of the trade newspaper *The Stage*. *The Stage* is a weekly publication aimed very much at theatre and television insiders in the main. Back in 1982, it was chock-full of adverts for the lesser, unaccredited drama schools. Too proud to ask anyone's advice, I decided to pick my drama school *blindfolded*. Not recommended.

One of the things that Studio '68 Principal Robert Henderson and his Polish vice-principal, Irwin Mayr, were obsessed with was theatre history; something I knew little or nothing about. And so, they gave me a few books and names to chew on; from the nineteenth century, Vselovod

Meyerhold, Ellen Terry, Henry Irving, Edward Gordon Craig and from
the twentieth century, Jerzy Grotowski, particularly his book *Towards a
Poor Theatre*; Peter Brook's *The Empty Space*; and Konstantin Stanislavski's
My Life in Art. Describing moments of enlightenment is a tricky business,
fraught with cliché and prosaic phrases. But I can truly say that reading
My Life in Art was like a light being turned on in my head, while a fire
was, simultaneously, lit in my heart. I lay on my bed and dreamt of
taking this career I had initially embarked on as a kind of sport, seriously –
suddenly feeling that this art *could* be spelt with a capital 'A'. It was a
memorable moment and one that changed the course and attitude of my
artistic life from that day onward. I'm not one, unfortunately, able to quote
liberally from the books I've read. But one phrase sticks in my mind from
Stanislavski's writings. It is his aphorism: *From conscious technique, to
the unconscious creation of dramatic truth*. That's been like a mantra
running through everything I've attempted since. Not always successfully,
sure, but I've had a hell of a lot of fun trying to live up to that challenge.
Trying to work out what a character means, why he does what he does;
what he might walk like, talk like, look like; what burns inside him, how
does he see the world around him; what are his longings and motivations.
And then, forgetting all that and walking like a blank sheet of paper on to
the stage – daring yourself to be painted with all the research and sculpting
you have been doing throughout the rehearsal period; trying, bravely, to
simply *be*.

Studio '68's old-school methods were pretty basic though and soon the
fact that it was an unaccredited drama school, run as a commercial repertory
company in order to keep it going, encouraged me to leave after only
eighteen months of the course. Amongst many of the advantages of the
school I had blindly plumped for was that the staff had the old-school
methods down to a T. I should like to take the space here to thank two great
teachers in particular: the late Rona Laurie and Richard Carey. Brilliant,
encouraging and thorough; the best part of my technique and stage-craft
comes from being taught by these two geniuses. Nevertheless, I knew I
needed the best training I could find, so took a year out to work for a firm
of solicitors, then applied to Britain's oldest drama school, the London
Academy of Music and Dramatic Art (LAMDA).

Entering LAMDA on my first day was as exciting as advertised in their
lavish prospectus. The school first opened in 1861, though it originally
solely catered for music students back then. It soon evolved into teaching
speech and then, naturally, drama. The technical theatre courses at LAMDA
are second-to-none. Those of us lucky enough to train there were spoilt
with a state-of-the-art theatre, the MacOwan, and a crew of technicians
who had no trouble finding work in the profession at the highest level.
Its reputation has only grown since the 1990s and LAMDA now boasts a
new theatre, housed in a brand-new faculty building, in the west of the
capital. Currently part of the Conservatoire of Drama Schools, LAMDA

trains hundreds of students, on its various technical and acting courses, as well as running an examinations board that is highly respected and has a global reach.

When I began attending in 1985, LAMDA had its main building on the Earls Court Road. In Tower House, large rehearsal rooms were graced with huge windows that offered a light and airy atmosphere to our daily regime of Alexander Technique, dance, clown, mask, movement, improvisation, Laban Technique and animal studies. I learnt much there that I still use today and I am very sure I would not have fared better at any other drama school. In fact, I had targeted just two – £15 a shot making it, of necessity, a limited venture. That rate is now £50 on average; a small fortune for the poorest applicants. LAMDA had the most eclectic choice of courses of all the drama schools I looked at and an emphasis on ensemble playing. Something that appealed to my egalitarian sensibilities. But there were some tricky moments at LAMDA, too.

One of the most memorable was the time when the entire year was ushered into a rehearsal room to hear what the faculty thought about our progress, or lack of it. It was a genuinely terrifying moment of vulnerability. A feeling of being about to be harshly criticized in an unloving, cruel way. Crushed somehow. To this day, I feel a foreboding every time there is a rehearsal note session. At LAMDA, after this particularly cruel and negative, public critique of my work, my nose began spontaneously gushing blood. I had to leave the room in front of twenty-three fellow students and the entire faculty. Never happened to me before or since. And not one of my drama school friends remember it happening. I suspect that's because they were all in abject fear that they'd be next.

My first professional role after LAMDA was in a new play written by Lucy Gannon, called *Raping the Gold*, for west London's Bush Theatre. Going to work as an actor for the first time was amazing. Here I was, cycling to work from Kensal Rise to rehearsals in Chiswick. Knowing that at the end of that week I would be receiving a wage packet of cash, to the tune of a whopping £160. My lord, was I happy. I would have done the job for a cup of tea and a cheese sandwich. True.

Luckily for me, play followed play for about two solid years. Then TV beckoned and I, reluctantly, got my first job on a children's serial called *Streetwise*. I say reluctantly, because my first love was really the theatre, so my then agent had to work ridiculously hard to get me to turn down playing Romeo at the New Victoria Theatre in Stoke.

In the subsequent years, I was fortunate enough to work with some great directors and many more wonderful actors. Men and women who have taught me more than I could ever say. Not just about acting and theatre, but about humanity, empathy and the acceptance of others. We're an odd bunch, actors, when one comes to think of it. Very few professions have active members ranging from birth to a hundred, from working class to upper class and across pretty much all ethnicities and sexual orientations. It makes it a forcibly eclectic grouping of randoms and leads, at best, to a healthy exchange of ideas and methods from one generation of practitioners to another. When I think of all the highways and byways that I could have gone down, I know, with absolute confidence, that I could not have chosen a better path.

3

The Royal Shakespeare Company

Before I write about our main subject, *Julius Caesar*, I'd like to say a little about my first stint at the Royal Shakespeare Company, way back in 1990. But first, for the uninitiated, a potted history.

* * *

There had been a theatre producing William Shakespeare's plays in Stratford-upon-Avon since 1879. In 1961, when under a youthful Peter Hall, it was given its royal charter, the site became the home of the newly-formed Royal Shakespeare Company (RSC). The desire for a permanent company of actors based in Stratford-upon-Avon, Shakespeare's birthplace and where the young William established a family life, had been a long-desired goal for the late Sir Peter, first artistic director of the newly-birthed and prestigious company. Arguably, the golden era for the proto-RSC came in the middle of the twentieth century, with actors like Sir Laurence Olivier, Sir John Gielgud and Dame Peggy Ashcroft. The African American superstar of the 1920s and 1930s, Paul Robeson, was to reprise his performance of Othello at Stratford; the second time he had played in England, the first being at the Savoy Theatre in London in 1930. He made his return as The Moor of Venice in 1959. The 1960s saw the RSC launching into modern takes on the Shakespeare canon. This culminated spectacularly in 1970/71 with Peter Brook's take on Shakespeare's *A Midsummer Night's Dream*.

This seminal production took the RSC, and British theatre tradition, through the looking-glass and all around the world. Brook's *The Dream* was staged in a white cube with trapezes hung from the 'flys' – that area in the rafters of a theatre where the lights and scenery live – from which the fairies, played by grown men for the first time, could make their entrances and exits. Brook exposed the workings of the theatre so that the stage-hands could be seen toiling above. No one had ever witnessed anything quite like this in British theatre. Nightmarish and disorientating. A psychedelic take, befitting the cultural explosion of the 1960s, Brook's production proved to a contemporary audience that Shakespeare was still vital and relevant, in a post-Moon-landing world.

The great actor Freddie Jones once told me about the moment at the end of Brook's *Dream* where all the actors leapt out into the auditorium to make their final exit, shaking hands with audience members. A shocking destruction of the famous 'Fourth Wall'. They were playing on Broadway in New York and, as he leapt off the stage, he all but stomped on Senator Edward Kennedy who, like a lot of spectators, was sitting in the aisle for want of a seat in the packed-out theatre. His story, of a post-show chat with Greta Garbo, was like hearing an echo from a lost era. Brook's *Dream* and his seminal book on the theatre, *The Empty Space,* greatly influenced theatre practice for at least the next fifty years. Brook's methods turned classic texts into blueprints for the exploration of modern ideas and new theatre practices. His boldest innovation, however, was the simplest and most poignant of ideas: in the final analysis, Brook suggested, nothing is needed for theatre to happen except a space for an actor to walk across with another person present to witness this act. Pure. Bare. Honest with a whiff of the absurd.

Subsidized to the tune of £18 million per year, through both governmental and private grants, the RSC holds a unique place in British theatre history and tradition. A theatrical hothouse, where young actors learn and hone their craft; where experienced performers become legendary names: Judi Dench, Kenneth Branagh, Diana Rigg, Jeffery Kissoon, Paul Scofield, Meera Syal, Antony Sher, Tamsin Greig, Joseph Marcell, Simon Russell Beale, Ralph Fiennes, Vanessa Redgrave, Mark Rylance, Nina Sosanya, David Tennant, Josette Simon and Lindsay Duncan. The RSC's repertoire of thirty-seven plays, sonnets and poems, is played out on a constant loop and has been for the past sixty years and more. They have also branched out, widening their remit to include classic plays from Shakespeare's contemporaries and modern twists to classical themes. With its royal patronage and international reputation for the purest verse-speaking, the RSC is the epitome of establishment theatre.

*　*　*

As mentioned at the close of the previous chapter, I was a theatre-lover first. But not just any theatre; political, heartfelt, preferably, non-commercial theatre. My first directors at the Cockpit Youth Theatre taught me that theatre is not just messing about in costumes, it is a potential force for social change. A teenager through the Margaret Thatcher years, my sense of being the last of the least as a working-class son of an immigrant, was strong. The class war was a real thing for me, not merely political theory. Allowing theatre to be seen by all, not just the privileged few, was vital in my eyes. The stories we told had to have social relevance for our time, I believed, and though I can now see the great merit of pure entertainment theatre, I still maintain that social-political relevance is where theatre will find its most vibrant life. After all, when we consider Shakespeare, his plays very often mirrored concerns and shifts in society at large, including the very highest echelons of British life.

Let's take a single example, *King Lear*, first performed in 1606. Shakespeare was presenting a play about the succession to the British throne and the dividing up of lands and loyalties, a mere three years after Queen Elizabeth I had passed away. The new king, James VI of Scotland, was a controversial figure for many. Him being crowned James I of England in 1603 made this transition from Tudors to Stuarts a time of great uncertainty and danger. Paranoia on all sides of the succession divide, the famous Gunpowder Plot, anti-Scottish sentiment and Scotland's long-standing alliance with France, Britain's ideological enemy, made for a tense period. Nevertheless, Shakespeare's newly anointed theatre troupe The King's Men didn't shy away from pinpointing, and indeed highlighting, the precise mood of the country. In *Lear*, an old king divides his kingdom between his three daughters and unleashes familial and civil strife, madness and destruction. If an establishment figure like Shakespeare could tackle such a delicate, potentially incendiary, theme as this at the start of the seventeenth century, despite the danger of accusations of disloyalty and sedition, then all the more reason why we in the twenty-first century, who have our much-vaunted freedom of speech, should be speaking truth to power.

Shortly before I left LAMDA, I felt strongly enough about theatre's purpose to say to a prospective, big-shot, agent that I did not want to leave drama school only to enter another institution like the RSC or the National Theatre. I would have preferred to work on good fringe and touring shows; theatre that would mean something to the people I was performing for. I think he nearly fell off his chair, before dismissing me as a misguided fool.

All this to say, that when the RSC first came knocking in 1990, I approached my auditions with great caution. My argument to my agent was: did I really need to get into a commercial machine like this so early on in my career? Yes, was the overwhelming response from friends and colleagues. I can see how strange this reluctance might seem to a young student now but you must remember that I was coming up at a time very much like the one in which I am currently writing.

Globally, political upheavals were being played out both on the right and the left on the world's stage. The right-wing, hawkish, Ronald Reagan in the USA; divisive, union-hating Tory, Margaret Thatcher, in the UK; the fall of the Berlin Wall the previous year, and my visits to Romania and the former Czechoslovakia in early 1989, were all part of the landscape of my practice at that time. The left-wing in the UK were subject to what amounted to a witch-hunt for 'reds' in the Labour Party, up and down the country. We students fought for the survival of the capital's Greater London Council, before it was dismantled, along with much arts and social funding; coal miners were beaten, brutally crushed and humiliated in the north; and the black community were often depicted as hopelessly criminalized and parasitical in the right-wing press. The riots and unrest amongst the black youth – suffering under the draconian 'sus laws', that had innocent children stopped and searched regularly by the police on their way to and from school – were a constant source of volatile tension. As students, we frequently marched against nuclear proliferation, South Africa's inhuman apartheid regime and the cutting of funding to our social institutions. When things are going well, when we are generally well-fed and entertained, these issues take a back seat. But such a time as I lived through in the 1980s and early 1990s may well be approaching us again. A potentially vibrant time for the Arts, perhaps. One hopes that theatre takes up the cause once again and uses its influence to speak out against injustices, intolerance and runaway greed.

With this mind-set, my acceptance into the RSC, a company whose commercial reputation was all-imposing, naturally left me in a quandary. The directors that I was being asked to work with and the plays I would be performing were truly impressive, however. My first audition was with Danny Boyle, then a theatre director who had done very little work behind camera. *The Last Days of Don Juan*, adapted by Nick Dear from the Tirso de Molina play, had a role that I longed to play: The Marquis de la Mota – a comic, foppish character, that I relished performing. Sam Mendes chose me for Shakespeare's *Troilus and Cressida*, which featured Ralph Fiennes in the title role and who I was to understudy, as well as playing Patroclus, loyal friend and cousin to Achilles – the excellent Cíaran Hinds. Getting to take over as Troilus for the final thirty or so performances was a great highlight of my early career. It was Sam's trust in my ability to keep a successful show going that gave me a hefty career leg-up. Next came *King Lear*, directed by the future artistic director of the National Theatre, Nicholas Hytner. I was to play Oswald; loyal, sneaky and venal servant to Lear's daughter, Goneril. And lastly, in the first part of a two-year season, RSC Artistic Director Terry Hands's production of *Love's Labour's Lost*. Playing Dumaine, alongside Ralph Fiennes and Simon Russell Beale, remains a lasting, joyful memory.

The gruelling first few months in Stratford-upon-Avon were tough and challenging. Rehearsing *Troilus* by day and performing *Don Juan* by night, followed by *Troilus* in the evening with daytime *Lear* rehearsals and, finally, *Lear* in repertory with the first two plays and *Love's Labour's Lost* rehearsals taking up my days. A marathon schedule that was later added to with a new adaptation of an early Henrik Ibsen play, *The Pretenders*, with Danny Boyle directing once more and me playing the lead role of young Norwegian king, Haakon Haakonsson.

Though the roles, actors, directors and plays were of the highest order, I was still struggling to believe in the work I was undertaking. So much of it seemed to function as another string in the sausage factory that was the RSC. A harsh take on a brilliant institution, it may be, but I was coming from a very different theatre discipline. I remember a conversation with the extraordinarily talented actor Sally Dexter, where she lamented the tourist-driven, chocolate-box staging of many of the shows. Sally and I were in three plays together, *King Lear, Don Juan* and *Troilus and Cressida*. Sally seemed to me to be asking why we were still performing Shakespeare in this traditional way. What was there to be gained from repeating what had been done for the last fifty years? Good questions, all of which I agreed we needed an answer to. However, trying to see the other side of things, I noted that theatre seemed to need to be both pure entertainment and informed, challenging debate. Not all productions could be like the ones staged by theatre company Cheek by Jowl – a troupe we had both previously worked with. Cheek by Jowl's take on Shakespeare's plays mirrored Peter Brook's from an earlier era. Their productions turned the expectations of the traditional theatre-going audience on their head. Certainly the best theatre company for actors who wanted to shake off the restraints of Shakespeare-as-museum-piece, that so many scholars and theatre critics seemed to want it to be.

In the defence of pure entertainment theatre, though, I had to point out to Sally that I had learnt a great deal from performing in *Love's Labour's Lost*. I hadn't really liked the play when I first read it. It seemed so staid, so un-dynamic. It is the story of four aristocratic friends, the King of Navarre and the three lords who are his closest friends, Berowne, Dumaine and Longaville. All three decide to be celibate for the space of three years in order to better devote themselves to fasting and study. The vows are broken within moments of the arrival of the Princess of France and her three ladies. The ensuing subterfuge, where the men pretend not to be in love with their respective ladies, is a tour de force of theatrical farce and audience collusion. I longed to do something original with Dumaine and asked the director, Terry Hands, if I could play him as an African prince. The Afro-British musical group Soul II Soul were huge in the UK at that time and a back-to-Africa notion was sweeping the young, urban, black populace. I felt that this approach was at least a nod to something that was actually happening in the real world, far away from Stratford's Royal Shakespeare Theatre (RST).

Terry denied me my choice, diplomatically. He suggested that, while my speeches in the gentle East African accent I had chosen were striking, the Edwardian England setting would not, perhaps, lend itself to this kind of interpretation. Back then, unfortunately, I was too ignorant to point out the very real, historical possibility of an educated East African being part of the entourage of these upper-class students in this period of British history. After all, the Sierra Leonean Classics scholar, Christian Cole, had graduated from Oxford University in the early 1870s; and he was not alone. The only idea I was allowed to keep was my change of costume, from Edwardian garb to East African robes. A cobbled together version of such robes, at least.

The biggest surprise for me, and the thing I wanted Sally to appreciate, was how the play itself, a rhyming-couplet orgy with farcical set-pieces and larger than life characters, could still pack a punch. A very tender, loving and life-affirming punch. I recall standing on the edge of the stage, wearing a mask that the play's heroes wear to disguise themselves, in the scene in which the lords try, in vain, to woo their ladies. This moment always embarrassed me in rehearsals and during the early previews. I felt uncomfortable with the artificial jollity and having to laugh at jokes only scholars and actors who had rehearsed the play for weeks could now understand. Obscure gags are one of the few millstones that Shakespeare has lumbered contemporary directors with. One day, however, I looked out into the auditorium during this scene and was astonished to notice a sea of faces looking up at the stage with expressions of pure delight and enraptured joy. If theatre can goad us into thinking, it can also soothe us with a sense of shared humanity. Entertainment, I realized then, was not a sin, but a necessity at times.

Troilus and Cressida in the beautiful, intimate, Swan Theatre, was dealing with the cases for and against armed conflict with a backdrop of the First Gulf War being played out in Iraq and Kuwait. Sam Mendes' production was spot-on in giving both sides of the intricate argument; all the while never allowing us to forget the cost of war. And here was gentle *Love's Labour's Lost*, next door in the RST, allowing us a breath of air before releasing us out into the maelstrom of the violent world outside. Two sides of the same coin. Two necessary and equally valid theatrical responses to the harsh realities of life.

Sally's real issue may well have been similar to mine. Stratford remains a very homogenous place, culturally and ethnically. The entire RSC company of eighty performers only included four black actors (two males and two females). And we were not represented at all in the technical departments. As a black boy from Willesden Green, Stratford was shockingly mono-cultural. I was stared at constantly on the street. I ignored it after a while but was always painfully aware that I was a curiosity. Another irritant for Sally and me was the obvious and old-fashioned hierarchy of the RSC structure; there were the stars and their single occupancy dressing rooms; the middle-rangers who shared with four others; and the so-called 'spear carriers', in dressing rooms for many more than that. 'Spear carrier' is an affectionate term for an actor who has been hired to play-as-cast, meaning you enter the RSC without a named role but you may later be assigned a role and a separate understudy role as the production progresses. If you were fortunate enough to land a sizeable understudy role, you could invite agents and casting directors as well as family and friends to watch the *understudy run*, usually held in the afternoon, complete with lights, costumes and sound. These actors, mostly young, were also prone to wildness due to their lack of focused occupation during the lengthy Stratford season. Long post-show sessions in the local pub, The Black Swan (aka The Dirty Duck), were a necessity for many of these budding Shakespeareans. Stories of actors behaving badly are legendary, so I need say no more. I largely avoided all of the excitement, however, as pub culture was never a part of my upbringing and I had just enough to occupy me with four plays and decent roles in each. All in all, for actors like Sally and me, who saw ourselves as class-warriors and politically conscious artists, it was a tough environment and one that either denuded you of your integrity or reinforced your determination to maintain it.

My lasting memories of that time are largely of feelings of isolation and otherness. The predominant culture of Oxbridge privilege left me in the cold. I did not have a lot in common with many of my fellow actors. But the work itself was my surest sanctuary. I learnt so much about myself and my art during those months. I may have suffered momentarily from a sense of disjointedness but that was worth it for the confidence and knowledge that I gained from this tough experience. It certainly rubbed the edges off many of my rather purist attitudes.

* * *

Well, perhaps not all my edges were smoothed by the RSC. After leaving there in the early months of 1992, I went directly into repertory with Nick Hytner's production of George Farquhar's *The Recruiting Officer* at the National Theatre. Several months of performing in what I increasingly began to feel was an empty production and I was convinced that theatre was no longer for me. That, in fact, acting may have exhausted its interest for me. Once again, I could not easily reconcile what I believed theatre could be with a system that seemed to me simply designed to churn out plays for the sake of keeping the audiences coming and sustaining yet another monolithic and impersonal institution. What was the point of theatre, I constantly wondered then, if its only remit is to give the audience what they want? Tradition, dressed up as contemporary art, in an arena that was overwhelmingly geared towards pandering to the white middle- and upper-classes. Where was the political edge I had grown to associate with theatre? What was the point of it all? Clearly, when one is in a negative frame of mind, everything is subject to this kind of unforgiving criticism.

I have never suffered a crisis quite like that one, thankfully, and I think it can be largely attributed to theatre-fatigue, brought about by months of relentless rehearsals and stage work. My salvation from this malaise came about through my next job. Gregory Hersov, then co-artistic director of the Royal Exchange Theatre in Manchester, was instrumental in preserving my spark of passion for the social and political possibilities of theatre. The play Gregory had been longing to do, ever since he was a young student, was James Baldwin's *Blues for Mr Charlie*. Set in a non-specific, southern America town, *Blues* was written by one of America's greatest writers at the height of the civil rights struggle in 1964. Our production, in a superb theatre-in-the-round setting, began with Manchester City Gospel Choir in the foyer, singing civil rights songs taken from that era. An eerie and powerful atmosphere enveloped the audience as the first scene – a flash-forward – ended with the shooting of my character, Richard Henry, by the southern

American town's most rabid racist. Richard's haunting last line before he is shot, 'You a man and I'm a man ... let's just get along', was an incendiary phrase to utter in a theatre packed with both the black and white communities of Manchester. Because of the intimacy of theatre-in-the-round, each community could see each other, too. Manchester at that time was a seething mess of racial tension. The town centre was noticeable in its lack of ethnic diversity; the Afro-British and British-Asian communities largely relegated to the Hume and Moss Side areas of the city. A little different now, of course, but back then the divide was real and palpable. Our question and answer event after the show was a powerful mix of town hall meeting and family therapy session. Each side was able to speak freely about racial tensions and address misunderstandings between different cultures and ethnicities. This was what theatre should be, I thought: personal, uncomfortable and meaningful to the spectators.

I had, at last, found my focus again. The RSC had to wait another twenty years before I would consider going back there once more. But when the offer came, it was absolutely irresistible.

* * *

Out of the blue, my agent suggested I have a chat with Gregory Doran, a theatre director I had met, informally, once or twice, but who I had never had the chance to work with. He wanted to discuss an idea he had been brewing for some time: a production of Shakespeare's *Julius Caesar* – set on the African continent – for the RSC. Greg proposed we set up a kind of symposium; gathering a group of actors, experts and RSC producers, to examine an African version of this well-worn play. I initially thought it odd that a long-standing associate director of the RSC, like Greg, needed in some way to prove that his idea of an African *Caesar* would work. Greg has since told me that the investigation was his idea, in order to clarify some of his own thoughts on this fresh take.

And so it was that a two-day symposium in July 2011 was arranged to interrogate Greg's vision. I was to read the part of chief conspirator, Marcus Brutus. The symposium would include lectures by Shakespeare historian Richard Wilson; the Julius Caesar expert Tom Holland; and journalist Martin Meredith, who had many years of experience covering areas of conflict on the African continent.

A cast of actors was assembled and our journey began.

4

Juliasi Kaizari:

Shakespeare's African Play

A few weeks before the symposium I'd had growing doubts relating to the appropriateness of the setting of Gregory Doran's *Julius Caesar*. It can be tempting to try to fit a square peg into a round hole in the theatre, especially when external agendas, social politics and the zeitgeist of present history are pushing this way or that. And so, it felt essential that we have a good reason for doing the play in this way and not simply for the kudos of having a politically correct, and long overdue, 'all black' production. The fact that the RSC had up to this point never had a production with an exclusively black cast couldn't be allowed to obscure the main question: is *Julius Caesar* a good fit for Africa?

Appropriately, Greg started our first morning by explaining why the idea of directing an African *Caesar* was such a burning desire of his. He told the story of the great Nelson Mandela and his fellow inmates on Robben Island and how imprisoned activist Sonny Venkatrathnam had smuggled a copy of the banned *Complete Works of Shakespeare* into the prison, hidden in the sacred Hindu text he was allowed to bring in. The book, assumed by the prison authorities to be the *Bhagavad-Gita* was, in fact, *The Complete Works of William Shakespeare* covered with greetings cards celebrating the Hindu festival Diwali. Members of the African National Congress then passed this precious work around and each inmate annotated their favourite sections. The play that proved to be the most popular was, of course, *Julius Caesar* and, crucially for our investigation, Nelson 'Madiba' Mandela's favourite quote was from one of Caesar's speeches. The great man had signed it, 'NRD Mandela 16-12-77'. The quote:

CAESAR
> Cowards die many times before their deaths
> The valiant never taste of death but once.
> Of all the wonders that I yet have heard
> It seems to me most strange that men should fear

Seeing that death, a necessary end,
Will come when it will come.

(*JC* 2.2.32–7)

Greg went on to tell of his trawl through various book websites, searching for two Shakespeare plays known to have been translated into Kiswahili by Tanzania's first president Julius Nyerere: *The Merchant of Venice* (*Mapebari wa Venisi*) and *Julius Caesar* (*Juliasi Kaizari*). Finding a copy of *Mapebari wa Venisi* for a few pounds, he promptly bought it and on opening the package discovered a dedication inside. It read, 'To Sir Laurence and Lady Olivier, kind regards, Julius Nyerere'.

By this time, the gathered actors were already intrigued by the African connections with the play that Greg had so far made. So the final line at the end of his conversation with the legendary Market Theatre of Johannesburg actor John Kani was almost a superfluous seal of approval on the whole venture. According to Greg, Kani told him that *Julius Caesar* is, quite simply, Shakespeare's African play.

The significance of John's quote cannot be overestimated. Johannesburg's Market Theatre was well known to us in the UK and US. We had the utmost respect for theatre movements that continued to produce high quality work in the face of the oppressive political environments they were forced to create in. The Market Theatre's repertoire of great plays was mostly written by the great Athol Fugard: *The Island, Siswe Banzi is Dead, Boesman and Lena, Master Harold and the Boys* and many others. A craftsman of the highest order, his was the voice we heard from the UK, informing us about the state of South Africa at that time – his writing a powerful, subtle protest that resonated around the world. It certainly satisfied my youthful attraction to politically conscious theatre.

Returning to the African translation: why did the remarkable leader Julius Nyerere, at the height of Tanzania's struggle for independence, feel the need to translate this most English of authors into Kiswahili?

Julius Kambarage Nyerere was known as 'Mwalimu', The Teacher, by all who knew him. He was the first Tanganyikan to receive a Master's degree after graduating from Edinburgh University in 1952. On his return, he gave up his teaching career and set about transforming the Tanganyika African National Union into a formidable force for independence from British rule. In 1962, he became the first president of the newly independent Tanganyika. After merging with Zanzibar, the fledgling African country was subsequently renamed the United Republic of Tanzania. Nyerere's ideas for advancing his people were simple, though revolutionary, ones: rely on self-sufficiency in your economy; take no money from the International Monetary Fund or the World Bank; and above all, rid yourself of colonial language. In this way you free the mind of your people to think independently. As a teacher, he believed education was key and *that* education, he insisted, should be in Kiswahili. Tanzania became the first country in Africa, after the end of colonial rule, to choose an African language as its national language.

Kiswahili, the language of the Eastern Coast, was spoken by a wide variety of peoples. It was a mixture of Bantu languages and Arabic and had been used as a trading language for hundreds of years. The fact that Nigeria, Ghana, Mali and Senegal, for example, all chose the colonial language as their national tongue, demonstrates how unique and far-sighted Mwalimu was. The unity that this brought to the more than one-hundred tribes in Tanzania, is evidenced by the relatively peaceful history it has enjoyed since the ending of British rule.

Mwalimu Nyerere tested this native language with the writings of the greatest exponent of creative writing that the colonists could offer: Shakespeare. He translated three plays into Kiswahili: *Macbeth*, *The Merchant of Venice* and, first, *Julius Caesar*. *Juliasi Kaizari* demonstrated the versatility of this African language – showcasing its ability to encompass the intricacies of the great original. Other African versions of the popular *Julius Caesar* include translations into several South African languages: Tsonga, Northern Sotho, Xhosa and Tshivenda. The best known version, however, is in Setswana by renowned South African writer and founding father of the African National Congress Sol. T. Plaatje, translated way back in the 1930s.

The interesting thing here is that Shakespeare was chosen as the epitome of Western literary and dramatic art. A sure-fire way to count yourself educated would be to know your Shakespeare. In fact, many African countries rejected outright – or treated with understandable suspicion – the literary canon of their old colonial oppressors. The books that might well survive would be, a la *Desert Island Discs*, the Bible and *The Complete Works of William Shakespeare*. So, in Nyerere's mind, a Kiswahili translation of a Shakespeare play would prove that this native language was capable of conveying the highest form of literary and artistic expression available in the Western world. A glittering prize, indeed, and one-in-the-eye of the old masters.

We may contrast Mwalimu's decision with the choice of the Kenyan leaders who, possibly, could not believe they'd resolve their national differences with the use of a lingua franca like Swahili. Nyerere saw the moral imperative as unity. Jomo Kenyatta of Kenya, perhaps less visionary, less interested in language than his neighbour down the coast, left his country to speak English as the official language and to simultaneously continue using their own native tongue.

One of the greatest African leaders the continent has ever known, Mwalimu was vilified, falsely, by the West, in the shape of the UK and the USA. The attacks on Nyerere's reputation, and the violence perpetrated on his soil, were a mark of his irritant-value to the West. The Organisation of African Unity had its headquarters in Dar es Salaam, as did other organizations from the Frontline States, highlighting Nyerere's status as a leader of integrity amongst these nations. He could count many great statesmen amongst his friends and admirers: Jomo Kenyatta (Kenya), Milton Obote (Uganda), Kwame Nkrumah (Ghana), Haile Selassie (Ethiopia) and Gamal Abdel Nasser (Egypt) to name just a very few. He hosted liberation movements, unwelcome and persecuted in their own countries – FRELIMO (Mozambique), MPLA (Angola), and the ANC of South Africa. The last word on Mwalimu Nyerere comes, fittingly, from Nelson Mandela:

I had the personal privilege of meeting him many years ago, in 1962, when I visited Tanzania seeking help as we embarked on the armed struggle. Then, as now, I was struck by his lucid thoughts; his burning desire for justice everywhere; and his commitment to Africa's interests.

After the independence of Tanzania, Mwalimu, as its head of state, continued to play an important role in the struggle for justice and democracy, not only in Africa but throughout the world.

On the basis of all this encouragement for an African reading of the play, our confidence grew that Greg knew precisely why this play needed to be seen in an African context. And the players who assembled to read the play that morning were, by this time, in total agreement with him.

The mirror of Caesar's story was clear: a charismatic leader, the legitimate source of national pride, disfigured by selfish ambition and avarice. Robert Mugabe of Zimbabwe, Idi Amin of Uganda, Ahmed Sekou Touré of Guinea – all of them fought for freedom from colonial rule and all succumbed to the seduction of power; silencing all opposition in the belief that they were the only ones who could unite their country. Not, as some lazy critics have tried, patronizingly, to suggest, that any of us thought it was the only African story, just a sadly common one.

* * *

As far as I can recall, we read *Julius Caesar* with very little preamble. Greg wanted to hear it without fuss or fanfare; and that was the first time I had an intuition he was something of a genius of clarity. There's nothing more telling than the first read-through and this one was no exception. Normally, what happens on first reading is that the more self-assured actors shine and the not-so-confident performers look a little tentative. But I've learnt not to be fooled by first impressions. Many a time as a younger actor, I had been frustrated at the lack of commitment I'd detected in my fellow actors during a read-through – too quiet, too slow – only to be shamed and blown away by their final performances, when the books are put away and their confidence has risen. However, something of the momentousness of this venture seemed to spur us all on. We read more and more passionately and the first intimations of the soul of the story – Brutus and Cassius' love – began to emerge. I'm not saying there isn't great love between Caesar and Antony but we only get one side of that. Caesar never mentions how he feels about Antony but Brutus and Cassius expose their feelings one for another throughout the play in various ways, positively and negatively. I believe the playwright's intent is that the love these two men have for each other should be the beating, human heart of the story.

The final scenes of the play affected me greatly and I knew, instantly, that there were hidden gems to be mined in it. At this stage, it is worth relating the Caesar story as told by William Shakespeare.

5

Shakespeare's *Julius Caesar*

Many versions of this story have existed for centuries. Somehow, though, only Shakespeare's version seems to have survived as a regularly performed play. Why might that be? The obvious answer would be his ability to bring the domestic to the momentous. His craft in putting into iconic characters' mouths words that not only explain their motivations but also the poetic turn of their thoughts. His lack of reverence, mixed with his utter respect for the humanity of his famous personalities, is what makes the plays seem accessible to us. In his skilful hands the great Caesar, Antony, Brutus and Cassius, Hamlet, Gertrude, Ophelia, Henry V, Macbeth, Cleopatra, Juliet, Romeo, princesses and princes, queens, commoners and kings, are brought to life as people first and historical-mythological characters second.

This particular play begins in an unexpected way; not with the great leader or his opponents but with two ordinary soldiers, disgusted at the crowd's celebration of Julius Caesar. These characters, Murellus and Flavius, are outraged that Pompey, their former leader, was once feted in this same way by this same crowd. The indignant soldiers accuse the mob of shameful fickleness; a charge that will come to haunt the play from beginning to end as the loyalties and factions in Rome are pulled this way and that. When this play is done well, the to-ing and fro-ing of loyalties is felt both onstage and in the auditorium.

The chastened citizens are then driven offstage by the angry soldiers. Once the crowd disperse, Caesar is introduced to us at the celebrations of the Lupercal: a ceremony that seemed to be a mixture of a sporting contest and political rally. Before Caesar can enter the arena, a Soothsayer calls out to him to 'Beware the ides of March.' The ides of March, the fifteenth, a calendar date that holds special, ominous significance in the play. Caesar's reply: 'He is a dreamer, let us leave him. Pass', will come to haunt him, as dreams take on a whole new significance in his conversation with his wife, Calphurnia, the morning of his assassination. In fact, the dream theme is laced throughout the play, as well as the idea of insomnia and, indeed, narcolepsy. Shakespeare loves to layer these thematic threads into his work, as he does with his next drama, *Hamlet*, where the theme of words and their meaning is constantly being highlighted, like subliminal advertising soaking into the audience's psyche. The later play, *Macbeth*, is suffused with the notion – though very sparingly used – of equivocation: the idea that we can say one thing and mean another. A frighteningly prescient vision of our contemporary political landscape.

Dismissing the mad Soothsayer, Caesar, with his friend and favourite Marc Antony, leaves with his train. Only Marcus Brutus and Caius Cassius remain; two men we have noticed only peripherally in the early exchanges. Our play truly takes off from here. Cassius, tightly-wound, angry and indignant at being passed over for high office, details the resentment he has for Caesar. Cassius is written as a straight-talking, fiery and openly emotional man. Brutus, the respected, so-called Stoic, is the prospective leader of the rebellion against the dictator. A Stoic is not, as many believe today, a person who believes in the subjugation of emotions by reason, but one who attempts to find a balance between the emotional and the rational, non-reactionary, quality in all intelligent, human decision-making. A Stoic, in Brutus' time, would have been seen as a wise and self-controlled person who does not allow themselves to act merely from emotions, but weighs their actions against the idea of an orderly natural universe. If nature, they might argue, is balanced and indifferent, humankind at its best should also strive to be. This is not so much a denial of emotions, more a philosophical method of coming to sane, natural and ethical decisions. Marcus Brutus is contained and cautious in Shakespeare's version though, importantly, not without a deep passion. Here is Plutarch on the differences between the character of Brutus and his friend Caius Cassius:

> This Brutus, of whom I now write, modified his disposition by means of the training and culture which philosophy gives, and stimulated a nature which was sedate and mild by active enterprises, and thus seems to have been most harmoniously tempered for the practice of virtue. As a consequence, even those who hated him on account of his conspiracy against Caesar, ascribed whatever was noble in the undertaking to Brutus, but laid the more distressing features of what was done to the charge of Cassius, who was a kinsman of Brutus, indeed, and his friend, but not so simple and sincere in his character.

Although nothing is settled in this first scene, we are left in little doubt that without Brutus any plot to change the status quo would be in grave trouble. Brutus is the unifying voice of reason, wisdom and legitimacy. Cassius, by contrast, has no such compunction to balanced argument and obsessively, viciously, relates a story that casts the great Caesar in an unmanly light:

CASSIUS
     ... For once, upon a raw and gusty day,
     The troubled Tiber chafing with her shores,
     Caesar said to me, '*Darest thou, Cassius, now*

Leap in with me into this angry flood,
And swim to yonder point?' Upon the word,
Accoutred as I was, I plungéd in,
And bade him follow, so indeed he did.
The torrent roared, and we did buffet it
With lusty sinews, throwing it aside . . .

But ere we could arrive the point proposed,
Caesar cried, *'Help me, Cassius, or I sink.'*

. . . And this man
Is now become a god, and Cassius is
A wretchéd creature, and must bend his body
If Caesar carelessly but nod on him.

(JC 1.2.100–18)

Brutus does not initially agree with Cassius' assessment of Caesar. As we'll see in an upcoming scene, he has a very complex relationship with Caesar that transcends the merely political or shallowly personal. His cautious reply, that Cassius must give him time to express his personal concerns, appeases his friend. But only temporarily.

BRUTUS
. . . Till then, my noble friend, chew upon this.
Brutus had rather be a villager
Than to repute himself a son of Rome
Under these hard conditions as this time
Is like to lay upon us.

(JC 1.2.170–4)

What a telling speech this is. After Cassius' bitter diatribe about Caesar, we get treated to the main focus of this play. The idea of the dignity of the free Roman citizen, unencumbered by tyrannical rule. We discover Brutus: a man torn between treason and subjugation. Brutus' final lines in this section are perhaps the most surprising for those who think of him as merely a cold Stoic. They give us a man sure of his cause, indignant at his nation's condition and fiercely proud of his noble ancestry. We learn in Plutarch, Shakespeare's Roman historian source, that the ancestors of Brutus helped defeat the Tarquin Kings, a royal dynasty that ended with the deposition of a hated tyrant. This call to his past will be the catalyst for action in Brutus' next scene. But here, surprisingly early on in the story, is a tough statement of intent for a man still apparently wrestling with his choices. And so, we see that Brutus is neither passive, nor overburdened with doubts; if anyone had overheard these words, they could well have accused Brutus of sedition on the spot.

Casca, a witty, cynical senator whose loyalties seem to be ambivalent, but whose sardonic take on the events inside the arena allows us insights into the wider political context that Cassius has touched on, offers us a window on the inner workings of the court of Caesar. He relates, in comic terms, how Antony tried to offer Caesar a crown. When the mob bayed against this, Caesar feigned his refusal of kingship. However, since the offer of the crown came three times it is implied by Casca that, in fact, Caesar and Antony were merely testing the waters of the crowd's hostility to a real coronation. We are left with the sense that the Lupercal was the beginning of Caesar's serious attempt at establishing a royal dynasty. An idea that is anathema to the ideals of a free Rome with free citizens.

There follows a storm, apparently full of supernatural signs according to Casca, when he relates the fierceness of the tempest to Cassius and the other conspirators. Later we'll find Caesar's wife, Calphurnia, reiterating these portents. The calmest place in the storm seems to be the garden of the potential chief conspirator Marcus Brutus. The stillness, however, belies the maelstrom of emotions that Brutus is going through. Shakespeare draws the picture of a man known as a Stoic in quite a different way from many previous versions of him. Not content to describe Brutus as those before him had, Shakespeare has Brutus suffer terrible torment in making his decision to murder Caesar. Alone onstage, Brutus cites, in a brilliant monologue, the reasons why he must act, and the argument leaves him drained but, finally, resolved to act:

BRUTUS
     It must be by his death. And for my part,
     I know no personal cause, to spurn at him,
     But for the general. He would be crown'd . . .

                                                    (*JC* 2.1.10–12)

The mere thought of crowning a man king is anathema to the ideals of Republican Rome. More than this, we can see immediately that the indignation of Brutus, unlike that of Cassius, is national rather than personal. The italics are mine:

BRUTUS
     . . . Crown him that,
     And then I grant we put a sting in him
     That at his will he may do danger with.
     The abuse of greatness is when it disjoins
     Remorse from power; and to speak truth of Caesar,
     I have not known when his affections swayed
     More than his reason.

                                                    (*JC* 2.1.15–21)

'The abuse of greatness is when it disjoins / Remorse from power.' Perhaps my favourite political line in all of the Shakespeare canon. So simple, but such a powerful thought. When power lacks a conscience it leads, inevitably, to abuses. A universal truth, along the lines of the famous aphorism in which absolute power corrupts absolutely. Now comes the moral compromise that Brutus has to make with an empirical actuality: '. . . and to speak truth of Caesar / I have not known when his affections swayed / More than his reason.' The pathologically honest Brutus has to admit that Caesar is never led by mere emotion, but is admirably balanced with rationality and reason, too. Shakespeare doesn't allow an easy answer for Marcus Brutus, forcing him to make a more precise case for the prosecution against Caesar. The story of humble aspiration is encompassed in the lines that follow, describing a climber turning his back on the ladder of ambition he has used to attain his goal. As if to say, that when the ambitious person attains the summit of their goals – to achieve great power – they instantly forget where they came from and humility goes out of the window. In the same way, to Brutus' mind, Caesar has forgotten that he is an ordinary man and not a god, as his behaviour seems increasingly to suggest he now thinks he is. Brutus advocates a preventative strike at the Man, Caesar, before he evolves into the Tyrant, Caesar, his nature and power threaten he might become. A tricky ethical conundrum. I asked myself these questions on a regular basis throughout my journey with the play: would it have been right to kill Adolf Hitler before he had taken power, for fear of what he *might* do? Would Hitler's murder – *before* a crime had taken place – been morally justifiable?

In Plutarch, the silencing of opposing voices is mentioned as' another cause for concern for the conspirators. In Shakespeare's play, both Murellus and Flavius, the outraged soldiers we met in the first scene, have been executed, along with many other dissenting voices. These factors give plenty of grist to Brutus' mill of indignation. Finally, the taunting nature of a note, thrown through his window, full of what Brutus calls 'instigations', makes matters personal; and not just related to the Republican ideal:

BRUTUS
   . . . Such instigations have been often dropp'd,
   Where I have took them up.
   '*Shall Rome, etc.*' Thus must I piece it out,
   Shall Rome stand under one man's awe? What Rome?
   My Ancestors did from the streets of Rome
   The Tarquin drive, when he was call'd a King.
   '*Speak, strike, redress.*' Am I entreated
   To speak, and strike? O Rome, I make thee promise,
   If the redress will follow, thou receivest
   Thy full petition at the hand of Brutus.

                          (*JC* 2.1.49–58)

The notes Brutus has received on a regular basis, admonishing him for his inaction, were almost certainly part of Cassius' plan to goad the cautious senator. This speech, in contrast to the previous one, is emotional-personal rather than philosophical-political. The real man is revealed in Shakespeare's brilliant style. Here is the passion, integrity and intelligence of Brutus. Ostensibly acceptable, even desirable, qualities for any politician, but in a political environment like Caesar's Rome, hopelessly idealistic. However, the goad that finally rouses Marcus Brutus to resolute action is one that recalls the brave and noble nature of his familial line: 'My ancestors did from the streets of Rome / The Tarquin drive, when he was called a King.' An intimation of that prideful fragility, a rigid quality that will be his ultimate downfall; his inability to see past honour, to the expedient, the secure, compromise.

Next come the conspirators Decius Brutus, Metellus Cimber, Cinna, Trebonius and Cassius. Brutus turns them away from their intent to kill Caesar's immensely popular favourite Antony, asking them to consider how it will look to the outside world:

BRUTUS

> Our course will seem too bloody, Caius Cassius,
> To cut the head off and then hack the limbs –
> For Antony is but a limb of Caesar.
> Let's be sacrificers, but not butchers, Caius . . .
>
> And for Marc Antony, think not of him,
> For he can do no more than Caesar's arm
> When Caesar's head is off.

(*JC* 2.1.161–82)

This coda, a dark joke indeed, is a mark of Brutus' confidence that what they are about to do is the right thing; that it will not be done out of jealously, or revenge, but out of a pure intent. Again, seeds of latent conflict are sown here, as Brutus has failed to listen to the other voices whose political views are more pragmatic, less esoteric, than his own. There is more than a hint of the blindly idealistic Brutus here, who thinks that his noble cause will shine through this brutal, premeditated murder.

The conspirators leave and, as if Brutus hadn't been through enough tonight, this intense, pivotal scene morphs into one that surprises us with an unexpected domesticity. The astonishing Shakespeare does not allow us to get carried away with the dryly historical Brutus but brings him right down to earth with a heart-rending bump. Brutus' wife, Portia, attempts to open Brutus up, desiring to hear the things that have been burdening him. He hasn't been sleeping, she reminds him, and his appetites have diminished. Perhaps, as with many people who are massively stressed, his physical affections have all but disappeared from their marriage, too. All signs that some great anxiety is weighing heavily upon him. She insists that they are equals. An immensely powerful claim for a female character to make on the English stage in 1599. The fact that the first actor to play Portia was, in fact, the only legal choice at the time, a boy, would not have made her statement of equality any less impactful. Given their equality, she insists, he should trust her with whatever is bothering him:

BRUTUS

> You are my true and honourable wife,
> As dear to me as are the ruddy drops
> That visit my sad heart.

PORTIA

> If this were true, then should I know this secret.
> I grant I am a woman but withal
> A woman that Lord Brutus took to wife.
> I grant I am a woman but withal
> A woman well reputed, Cato's daughter.
> Think you I am no stronger than my sex,
> Being so fathered and so husbanded?
> Tell me your counsels, I will not disclose 'em.

> (*JC* 2.1.287–97)

Her *coup de grâce* is to show Brutus a cut she has made in her thigh, a demonstration of how stoical *she* can be. A form of self-harming that completely disarms Brutus who practically breaks down at the end of this marathon scene; a scene that has included his own doubts, his sleepy servant, Lucius, and a gang of men hell-bent on murder.

BRUTUS

> O ye gods.
> Render me worthy of this noble wife.
> Hark, hark, one knocks. Portia, go in a while,
> And by and by thy bosom shall partake
> The secrets of my heart . . .
> Leave me with haste.

> (*JC* 2.1.301–7)

And, steeling himself to lead once again, Brutus persuades an old senator, Caius Ligarius, to join him in the planned assassination. Brutus ends this sequence re-energized and focused, a sharp contrast from the man who began the scene.

And so to the morning of the assassination and this fast-moving play has us in Caesar's house hearing the great leader's insomnia-driven thoughts:

CAESAR

> Nor heaven nor earth have been at peace tonight.
> Thrice hath Calphurnia in her sleep cried out,
> 'Help, ho. They murder Caesar.'

(JC 2.2.1–3)

Calphurnia has more to say on the subject of supernatural portents, when she finds him up and ready to go to the Senate:

CALPHURNIA

> ... A lioness hath whelpéd in the streets,
> And graves have yawn'd, and yielded up their dead.
> Fierce fiery warriors fight upon the clouds
> In ranks and squadrons, and right form of war
> Which drizzled blood upon the Capitol ...
>
> O Caesar, these things are beyond all use,
> And I do fear them.

(JC 2.2.17–26)

But this is Caesar and whilst we have heard that his night has been disturbed, his determination not to appear cowardly drives the following speech; Madiba's favourite:

CAESAR

> Cowards die many times before their deaths,
> The valiant never taste of death but once.
> Of all the wonders that I yet have heard,
> It seems to me most strange that men should fear,
> Seeing that death, a necessary end,
> Will come when it will come.

(JC 2.2.32–7)

One wonders what thoughts this domestic row brought up for Nelson, as he contemplated similar conversations he may well have had with his wife Winnie Mandela, before and during his long incarceration. For Caesar, Calphurnia's fears seem almost to act as an incentive for him to brave fate. He even dismisses the bad auguries of an animal sacrifice that – on disembowelment – exposed a literally heartless beast. Then – as Portia did in the previous scene – Calphurnia takes to her knees. The effect is immediate. Suddenly, Caesar yields to her wishes. Clearly, for women in this society, the ace up the sleeve in a critical debate is kneeling in supplication before their husbands. And just as obvious, it is the husband's duty to accede to pretty much anything their wife desires at that point. One has to ask oneself where the power truly lies, then, in a relationship where one partner, by 'going to ground', has the upper-hand guaranteed. Upon entering, conspirator Decius Brutus insists on knowing the true cause of Caesar's determination that he simply 'Will not go.' And here we see how clever Decius stokes the dormant fires of Caesar's ambitions:

DECIUS BRUTUS
>   This dream is all amiss interpreted.
>   It was a vision fair and fortunate.
>   Your statue spouting blood in many pipes,
>   In which so many smiling Romans bathed,
>   Signifies that from you great Rome shall suck
>   Reviving blood . . .
>   This by Calphurnia's dream is signified.

(*JC* 2.2.83–90)

Pressing his advantage home, Decius concludes with this final appeal to Caesar's over-sized ego:

DECIUS BRUTUS
>   . . . The Senate have concluded
>   To give this day a crown to mighty Caesar.
>   If you shall send them word you will not come,
>   Their minds may change. Besides, it were a mock
>   Apt to be rendered, for someone to say,
>   'Break up the Senate till another time,
>   When Caesar's wife shall meet with better dreams.'
>   If Caesar hide himself, shall they not whisper,
>   'Lo Caesar is afraid'? . . .

CAESAR
>   How foolish do your fears seem now, Calphurnia.
>   I am ashaméd I did yield to them.
>   Give me my robe, for I will go.

(*JC* 2.2.93–107)

Shakespeare's skill is evident here in the way he contrasts the domestic life of the Dictator with that of the Stoic. Brutus talks lovingly, emotionally even, to his wife and gives her the license to speak into his situation. Caesar gives no such latitude to Calphurnia but rather treats her like an irritant and completely ignores her, not even deigning to give her a farewell, once the conspirators and Antony arrive to accompany him to the Senate. Thus is set in motion the mechanisms for the destruction of the greatest leader Rome had ever known.

Next, we meet a loyal subject, Artemidorus, who is busy composing a note to Caesar, giving away the names and intent of the conspirators.

Shakespeare adds this layer of suspense to increase the tension we're already feeling. And he gives us one more layer of personal tension, before we get the inevitable assassination scene. Portia is losing her mind with worry and stress. She orders their servant boy, Lucius, to find out how her husband is faring, yet keeps stopping him, even as he tries to leave to seek his master in the Capitol. When the Soothsayer from the first act appears, on his way to the Capitol, Portia tries to find out why *he* needs to speak to Caesar. Receiving the obtuse answer that he must warn Caesar of harm that he fears 'may chance', Portia's worries are only exacerbated and her parting lines are full of confusion, fear and a touch of Lady Macbeth-ian madness:

PORTIA
> I must go in. Ay me. How weak a thing
> The heart of woman is. O Brutus,
> The heavens speed thee in thine enterprise.
> Sure the boy heard me. Brutus hath a suit
> That Caesar will not grant. O, I grow faint.
> Run, Lucius, and commend me to my lord,
> Say I am merry . . .

(JC 2.4.40–6)

The most famous assassination in history is the violent climax to the next scene, though Shakespeare is in no particular hurry to get there. He treats us to an additional couple of moments of theatrical tautness, where we see the gathering conspirators closing in on Caesar, only to have their plans interrupted by the loyal Artemidorus, bringing Caesar word of the murderous conspiracy. An arrestingly modern exchange of tense lines follows in a high-pressure moment for all the characters. Caesar, anticipating his coronation, the conspirators, poised to strike him down and fearing exposure before the act:

ARTEMIDORUS
> Hail, Caesar. Read this schedule.

DECIUS BRUTUS
> Trebonius doth desire you to o'er-read,
> At your best leisure, this his humble suit.

ARTEMIDORUS
> O Caesar, read mine first, for mine's a suit
> That touches Caesar nearer. Read it, great Caesar.

CAESAR
> What touches us ourself shall be last served.

ARTEMIDORUS
>   Delay not, Caesar, read it instantly.

CAESAR
>   What, is the fellow mad?

PUBLIUS
>   Sirrah, give place.

CASSIUS
>   What, urge you your petitions in the street?
>   Come to the Capitol.

                                                        (*JC* 3.1.3–12)

Ridding themselves of Artemidorus, the conspirators are free to stage events so that Caesar's megalomania is witnessed very publicly and at its height, moments before they murder him. They stir him to indignation, by encouraging fellow-conspirator Metellus Cimber to petition for his banished brother's pardon. As all the conspirators join in the chorus demanding mercy, Caesar finally lets rip and shows us a man with high ideals and a self-confidence that contradicts the cautious, even fearful, man of his previous domestic scene:

CAESAR
>   . . . I am constant as the northern star,
>   Of whose true-fixed and resting quality
>   There is no fellow in the firmament.

>   . . . and that I am he,
>   Let me a little show it, even in this –
>   That I was constant Cimber should be banishéd,
>   And constant do remain to keep him so.

                                                        (*JC* 3.1.60–73)

This is Caesar's last full speech. What follows is the brutal, violent and bloody murder of the great man. His speechifying ends with that most notorious of all lines in *Julius Caesar* – made famous it is believed by Shakespeare, rather than his historical source for the story, Roman historian Plutarch – 'Et tu, Bruté?' It has been suggested that Shakespeare had read that other great Roman historian, Suetonius, who mentions witnesses who claimed Caesar spoke these words, or similar ones, at the time. But no body of evidence exists to support the Suetonius claim and, in any case, it is Shakespeare's line that we remember. A great example of the power of art to render history into vivid life and, curiously, to turn fiction into fact. The full line in *Julius Caesar* is:

CAESAR
    Et tu, Bruté? Then fall, Caesar.

(JC 3.1.77)

After the panicking Senators, who had not been part of the conspiracy, have
fled, Brutus urges his followers on to an act that might seem cruel to us but
was the most honest, inspiring gesture Brutus could think of to mark this
momentous victory. Incidentally, I also love the idea contained in Cassius'
lines that we, who live two-thousand years after the event, will speak about
it in accents not known to Roman society at the time:

BRUTUS
    Stoop, Romans, stoop,
    And let us bathe our hands in Caesar's blood
    Up to the elbows, and besmear our swords,
    Then walk we forth, even to the market-place,
    And waving our red weapons o'er our heads,
    Let's all cry: Peace, freedom, and liberty.

CASSIUS
    Stoop then, and wash. How many ages hence
    Shall this our lofty scene be acted over
    In states unborn and accents yet unknown.

(JC 3.1.105–13)

The conspirators begin to smother their swords with the blood of the dead
man; a far cry from the words Brutus had spoken earlier in his garden: 'Let's
be sacrificers, but not butchers, Caius.'

A tense stand-off with the grieving Antony is the hyper-tense, penultimate
beat of this epic scene. Before Antony's entrance, the conspirators urge
Brutus to murder Antony, too, but he demurs; preferring to try to reason
with him. A mistake or an act of true integrity? Only the unfolding events
will tell. In Plutarch, the subsequent incidents are separated into the days
that followed the assassination but Shakespeare, ever mindful of theatrical
pacing, truncates these into a single moment to dazzling effect. One great
example of Shakespeare's divergence from his source is the moment when
Antony shakes the bloody hands of each conspirator. We shudder at the
thought of what this must feel like for a brave, noble and fierce warrior like
Antony who has just gazed upon the bloody, butchered corpse of his friend
and leader. One by one, meticulously, Antony shakes the hand of every
murderer there. As the conspirators leave the scene clear for Antony to
mourn his friend, we may feel that the assassination has accomplished
precisely what Brutus might have dreamt it would: a peaceful transition of
power from Caesar and Antony to Brutus and Cassius. But that would be
too easy. Shakespeare has us observe a rather sketchy character, seen only

very fleetingly up until now, transform himself into an avenging angel, through one of the finest speeches in the English language:

ANTONY

    O, pardon me, thou bleeding piece of earth,
    That I am meek and gentle with these butchers.
    Thou art the ruins of the noblest man
    That ever livéd in the tide of times.
    Woe to the hand that shed this costly blood.
    Over thy wounds now do I prophesy . . .

    A curse shall light upon the limbs of men,
    Domestic fury and fierce civil strife
    Shall cumber all the parts of Italy.
    Blood and destruction shall be so in use,
    And dreadful objects so familiar,
    That mothers shall but smile when they behold
    Their infants quartered with the hands of war . . .

    And Caesar's spirit, ranging for revenge . . .

    Shall in these confines with a monarch's voice
    Cry 'Havoc', and let slip the dogs of war . . .

                                    (*JC* 3.1.254–73)

Sending his servant to speak to Octavius Caesar – Julius' great-nephew according to Plutarch and named in Caesar's will as his successor – Antony details his plans for his next move. He will, having already won Brutus' permission, address the people in the market place in hopes of turning them against the conspirators.

    This is the usual point at which a production of *Julius Caesar* has an interval. A neat end to this chapter, too, I think.

6

Julius Caesar, Part Two

The Forum Scene that follows is the most famous in *Julius Caesar,* apart
from the assassination itself. Brutus does his best to quieten the crowd and
reasons with them about the justness of the conspirators' cause. He is an
excellent orator, respectful of their intelligence and integrity. He seems to
leave them satisfied of his righteousness. He even persuades them, against
their will, to listen to Caesar's closest ally and friend, Marc Antony. Antony
surprises us all with his skills of oratory, completely winning the crowd to his
cause and triggering the violent rebellion that ensues. How could they have
resisted a man who, before their eyes, weeps over the blood-soaked corpse of
his friend; who shows them the vicious wounds the conspirators carved into
Caesar's flesh; and who speaks to them in powerful, emotive phrases?

ANTONY
> Friends, Romans, countrymen, lend me your ears.
> I come to bury Caesar, not to praise him.

> *(JC 3.2.74–5)*

A clever opening, in which Antony, brilliantly wielding the rapier of oratory
while claiming to be no orator, manipulates a skittish mob. The three pillars
of Rhetoric: pathos, ethos and logos, all turned to his manipulative use in
these two, brief opening salvos. Within moments, Marc Antony turns the
mob's former hatred of Caesar to tears of regret at his passing. The killer
blow is Antony's reading of Caesar's will, which purports to give so
generously to the people of Rome. The resultant reaction is almost inevitable:

PLEBIAN 3
> Most noble Caesar. We'll revenge his death.

PLEBIAN 4
> O royal Caesar.

ANTONY
> Here was a Caesar. When comes such another?

PLEBEIAN
> Never, never. Come, away, away.
> We'll burn his body in the holy place,
> And with the brands fire the traitors' houses.

(JC 3.2.236–46)

In a brief and darkly poignant moment after the famous Forum Scene, we meet a lone poet, Cinna, caught in the wrong place at the wrong time. Antony's oratory has left us roused and indignant. Despite what we have seen and heard about Caesar, we can't help but be carried away with Antony's brilliance. Shakespeare knows this, luring us into a false sense of righteous indignation, only to turn the tables on us immediately. He has the innocent poet, the unluckily named Cinna, slaughtered by a violent mob who mistake him for the conspirator of the same name. In this way, Shakespeare asks us the question, 'How can we be sure we are being swayed by reasoned argument and not by clever words and a mob mentality?' A question that is still as relevant today as it was in Caesar's or Shakespeare's day. A warning to listen carefully, weighing the words we are being spun; to examine forensically the truth that is being offered to us. The murder of Cinna is a reminder that a mob incited to violence is an impersonal machine once unleashed. This mob moves on to attack the houses of all the known conspirators. Brutus and Cassius flee. Civil war has begun.

A three-way leadership, the Triumvirate, is briefly in focus for the next phase of the play. Lepidus, Octavius and Antony vie for power. Antony dismisses Lepidus as insignificant, focusing the defiant young gun Octavius' attention on bringing down the fleeing Cassius and Brutus. We learn, too, that Antony had lied to the mob, merely pretending to read Caesar's will verbatim. We may now look back at that Forum Scene and see it in a more sinister light.

Now, and for the rest of the story, Shakespeare focuses on the most important relationship in the play, Brutus and Cassius. Our next port of call is Brutus' tent in the fields of Sardis. Brutus clearly has a grudge against Cassius but tries to hold it back. Cassius, ever honest, charges straight into an argument about a corrupt soldier not pardoned by Brutus, though Cassius had specifically asked for this favour. Brutus' anger erupts and all his seething resentments are unleashed. This is a new Brutus, a Brutus even Cassius has never seen. A man of fiery indignation, of barely controlled passion and rage:

BRUTUS
> Remember March, the ides of March remember.
> Did not great Julius bleed for justice' sake?
> What villain touched his body, that did stab
> And not for justice? What? Shall one of us,
> That struck the foremost man of all this world

But for supporting robbers, shall we now
Contaminate our fingers with base bribes? . . .
I had rather be a dog, and bay the moon,
Than such a Roman.

(JC 4.3.18–28)

Violence seems to be in the air, until Cassius, not for the first or last time in the play, threatens to take his own life there and then. Brutus, having goaded Cassius to this extremity, barely prevents him from stabbing himself and a kind of exhausted calm ensues. A poet enters demanding that the two men make peace. Brutus, uncharacteristically again, violently ejects the poet and the two kinsmen are alone, at last. The next beat of this powerful scene has them sharing their most honest moment together as Brutus makes a heart-breaking revelation:

CASSIUS
I did not think you could have been so angry.

BRUTUS
O Cassius, I am sick of many griefs.

CASSIUS
Of your philosophy you make no use,
If you give place to accidental evils.

BRUTUS
No man bears sorrow better. Portia is dead.

CASSIUS
Ha? Portia?

BRUTUS
She is dead.

(JC 4.3.141–7)

Brutus tells how Portia had been pining for his absence and that news of Antony and Octavius' successes had reached Rome at the same time. Fearing the worst, she had dismissed her servants and, swallowing hot coals, taken her own life. A noble Roman end for this most remarkable of Roman women. Brutus refuses to speak more of his grief and asks his servant, Lucius, to bring them wine with which they may pledge love to one another:

BRUTUS
Speak no more of her. Give me a bowl of wine.
In this I bury all unkindness, Cassius.

CASSIUS
> My heart is thirsty for that noble pledge.
> Fill, Lucius, till the wine over-swell the cup.
> I cannot drink too much of Brutus' love.

(*JC* 4.3.156–60)

Moments later, two close allies, Titinius and Messala, confer with Brutus and Cassius about their next military move. Cassius favours waiting till Antony and Octavius come to them, Brutus is for the opposite course of action, wanting to surprise the enemy at Philippi; a plan that may well exhaust his own soldiers in the executing, as Cassius implies. Brutus believes their allies to be at the height of their powers, while any delay only gives Antony and Octavius time to grow even stronger. He finally wins the fiery Cassius over with the following rousing speech:

BRUTUS
> Our legions are brimful, our cause is ripe,
> The enemy increaseth every day,
> We, at the height, are ready to decline.
> There is a tide in the affairs of men,
> Which taken at the flood, leads on to fortune,
>
> ... On such a full sea are we now afloat,
> And we must take the current when it serves,
> Or lose our ventures.

(*JC* 4.3.213–22)

Cassius, his love for Brutus again outweighing his military nous, agrees. A decision that will lead to their ultimate downfall. Left alone, Brutus sees a vision of the dead Caesar, warning him that he will see him again at Philippi. Snapping into reality, Brutus orders his men to prepare to march out.

A series of jagged, military scenes follow, with standoffs and posturing on both sides. We witness an oddly poignant aside (a theatrical term for a private conversation onstage) as Cassius tells Messala that it is his birthday. He also reiterates that he did not agree with Brutus' plan to battle here at Philippi. On top of his own military misgivings about that decision, the signs and portents he has witnessed have led him to conclude that today may well be his last. Cassius makes mention of a moment found in Plutarch, where the conspirators' ensign, the equivalent of a standard, the flag that troops rally around and attempt to defend at all costs, attracts two eagles. This play is packed with references to animals and nature affecting human affairs. Cassius has noted that the eagles have flown, to be replaced by 'ravens, crows and kites', carrion-eating birds all. His final exchange with Brutus is so subtly emotional that it could well be overlooked in its significance. But, if we read between the lines (subtext in acting terms) we can feel the pain, love and resignation to fate both men feel but cannot, publicly, articulate:

CASSIUS
 ... But since the affairs of men rest still incertain,
 Let's reason with the worst that may befall.
 If we do lose this battle, then is this
 The very last time we shall speak together.
 What are you then determinéd to do?

(*JC* 5.1.95–9)

It appears that Cassius is asking Brutus if he will, like a noble Roman, commit suicide rather than submit to Antony and Octavius. The Cato mentioned in the following speech was Brutus' father-in-law, the father of Portia, who committed suicide rather than submit to his enemies. Shakespeare goes directly against Plutarch's reading of Brutus' attitude to suicide, giving him a more negative, though convoluted, stand against it. Although, it must be noted, these two generals are speaking very publicly before their respective soldiers:

BRUTUS
 Even by the rule of that philosophy
 By which I did blame Cato for the death
 Which he did give himself – I know not how,
 But I do find it cowardly and vile,
 For fear of what might fall, so to prevent
 The time of life – arming myself with patience
 To stay the providence of some high powers
 That govern us below.

 ... And whether we shall meet again I know not.
 Therefore, our everlasting farewell take.
 For ever, and forever, farewell, Cassius.
 If we do meet again, why, we shall smile,
 If not, why then this parting was well made.

CASSIUS
 For ever, and forever, farewell, Brutus.
 If we do meet again, we'll smile indeed,
 If not, 'tis true this parting was well made.

(*JC* 5.1.100–21)

It feels so tight, so buttoned up, this conversation between two men who love each other as fiercely as brothers. But here, beneath the gaze of their

troops, they cannot speak more intimately than this. When, at the end of the
play, we look back on the events that follow, we may come to realize that
this was their very last conversation. The next scenes take place in the heat
of battle, where we find Cassius and his men Pindarus and Titinius fleeing
Antony's troops who have apparently taken Cassius' camp. Alone, briefly,
Cassius reveals his thoughts to us:

CASSIUS
> This day I breathéd first: time is come 'round,
> And where I did begin, there shall I end.
> My life is run his compass.

> > > > > > > > > > > (*JC* 5.3.23–5)

Cassius sends Titinius to verify if the troops they can see near Cassius' tents
are allies, or enemies. Pindarus is ordered to the top of the nearby hill to
report to the exhausted Cassius what he sees. And with the news that Titinius
is taken by the enemy, Cassius persuades Pindarus to kill him and receive his
promised freedom. Pindarus obeys and Cassius dies at the hands of his, now
liberated, loyal servant. The tragic truth is that Pindarus has mistaken events.
What looked like enemy soldiers surrounding Titinius were, in fact, allied
troops congratulating him on Cassius' victory. The defective vision of
Pindarus has misinterpreted what was happening in the field before him.
Adding extra irony to his unnecessary death, at this point in the battle,
Brutus is in the ascendancy. When he finally reaches Cassius' body, Brutus
ends the scene with a moving tribute to his friend:

BRUTUS
> . . . The last of all the Romans, fare thee well.
> It is impossible that ever Rome
> Should breed thy fellow. Friends, I owe more tears
> To this dead man than you shall see me pay.
> I shall find time, Cassius, I shall find time.

> > > > > > > > > > (*JC* 5.3.99–103)

Alas, he never does. Events now rush headlong towards our finale as Brutus
rouses his troops to one more push. The final scene has Brutus sensing the
end is near. That being the case, he is determined to take the Roman way and
end his life by what he considers noble means: assisted suicide. In a scene
charged with pathos, the broken leader of men tries to talk his closest friends
into killing him as Pindarus did for Cassius. Mildly irritating, perhaps, for
an exhausted audience, Shakespeare now introduces us to several characters
we are unfamiliar with. It is to his great credit, however, that the power of
the scene supersedes our natural fatigue at the end of this emotionally potent
play. As the soldiers Dardanius and Clitus won't perform this act, the
weeping Brutus then asks Volumnius:

BRUTUS
   ... I know my hour is come.

VOLUMNIUS
   Not so, my lord.

BRUTUS
   Nay, I am sure it is, Volumnius.

   ... Thou know'st that we two went to school together;
   Even for that our love of old, I prithee
   Hold thou my sword-hilts, whilst I run on it.

VOLUMNIUS
   That's not an office for a friend, my lord.

                    (*JC* 5.5.20–9)

After dismissing his men, Brutus, desperate though he is, holds to his earlier promise to Cassius not to commit suicide by his own hand and wakes a sleeping servant, Strato, ordering him to hold his sword while he throws himself on the blade tip. Our flawed hero Marcus Brutus keeps his integrity even *in extremis*. Dying, the haunting image of Caesar seems to appear to his mind's eye:

BRUTUS
   Caesar, now be still,
   I killed not thee with half so good a will.

                    (*JC* 5.5.51–2)

After the noble Brutus' death, Antony and Octavius enter. Torn between victory and sorrow, the final lines of the play are shared between the respectful Antony and the ambitious youth, destined to become one of the greatest leaders Rome will ever know: Octavius 'Augustus' Caesar.

ANTONY
   This was the noblest Roman of them all:
   All the conspirators, save only he,
   Did that they did in envy of great Caesar;
   He, only in a general honest thought
   And common good to all, made one of them.
   His life was gentle, and the elements
   So mixed in him that Nature might stand up
   And say to all the world, *'This was a man!'*

OCTAVIUS
> According to his virtue let us use him,
> With all respect and rites of burial.
> Within my tent his bones tonight shall lie,
> Most like a soldier, ordered honourably.
> So call the field to rest, and let's away,
> To part the glories of this happy day.

(JC 5.5.69–82)

And with that rather false-note of a closing line ringing, bitterly, in our ears, the play ends.

7

Symposium

According to Greg Doran, Richard Wilson, Shakespeare expert and author of *Shakespeare: Julius Caesar*, and Tom Holland, writer of *Rubicon*, the story of Caesar's triumphant entry into Rome as conqueror, were both already converts to the idea of a production of *Julius Caesar* set in Africa. Martin Meredith, a journalist who had decades of experience covering many post-independence African countries, on the other hand, might need some convincing. This seemed to be an ideal set-up for an honest debate.

At the start of day two of the symposium, Tom Holland spoke about the subject of his book, *Rubicon*. He described in forensic detail the state of Rome at the time of Caesar's audacious and successful attempt to become the supreme leader of the great empire. Suddenly, I felt a surge of doubt again. Despite Greg's rousing tales the previous day, the story now felt so Western, so specifically Roman. I struggled anew to see how it could fit an African context. That worry was not allayed when Richard Wilson, our resident Elizabethan historian, spoke at length about Shakespeare having written the play during a period of national crisis in England. A time when the tensions surrounding the succession to the childless Elizabeth I's throne was at its height.

But then, just as I was leaning on the side of really questioning the wisdom of the idea, to my relieved surprise, the apparently most-sceptical-person-in-the-room, Martin Meredith, became the fiercest advocate of them all for setting *Julius Caesar* in Africa. Martin told us how time after time in many colonial African countries he had worked in, a strong man, a warrior, would rise, be persecuted by the colonial authorities, only to emerge as a triumphant leader. Freedom would ensue and then, inevitably, the consolidation of power. A dictator would be born out of the desire for stability, the death knell of a fledgling democracy would sound. An all too familiar tale for many post-independence African nations.

On the final afternoon, we were due to read the play again in front of leading figures at the RSC. Our audience would include, amongst others, the journalist Yasmin Alibhai-Brown, who was to be our facilitator for any post-reading discussions; John Wyver, head of Illuminations, a film company that had previously shot Greg Doran's *Macbeth*, starring Sir Antony Sher and Dame Harriet Walter, as well as his *Hamlet*, starring David Tennant; and finally, the artistic director of the RSC, the innovative Michael Boyd. There seemed to suddenly be an awful lot riding on our performances in this public read-through of the play; consequently, we could all feel the mounting tension.

So, it was with care that I approached Greg at lunchtime and asked if I could try a mild, East African accent. He hesitated and I could see how nervous he felt about it: the subtext being that it had gone very well thus far, so did we really need to spoil it with an added challenge for our audience? I can't second guess his true thoughts, naturally, but I could see how one might be nervous of the board's reaction to accented Shakespeare. It's all right for a company like, say, Northern Broadsides to accent Shakespeare, but is it really acceptable for the country's leading exponent of the works of the great man? Northern Broadsides, a company founded by actor Barry Rutter, prides itself on wresting Shakespeare from the hands of *posh* theatre tradition and has been a vital source of earthy, authentic Shakespeare productions since 1992. Rutter's productions have led the way in breaking the stranglehold of the Oxbridge School of Shakespeare; delivering the plays in an accent easily familiar to the largely northern, British audiences that view them. An enormously important company, Northern Broadsides has been the forerunner for many a production in the mainstream theatre, where regional accents had traditionally been seen as the voice of working-class characters in Shakespeare, exclusively.

My take on accents in Shakespeare is this: since, in Shakespeare's time, the majority of people, of whatever class, spoke in what would now be called a regional accent, with hard 'R's, flat 'A's, and in some cases a country burr, then how can we say with any true accuracy what Shakespeare's actors would have sounded like? Not *posh*, that's for certain, and not what we would now call Standard English, BBC English or the more formal term, Received Pronunciation (RP). According to linguist David Crystal in his excellent book *The Stories of English*, RP was little known before the very late 1700s and not standardized till much later. Regional dialects in speech were a normal and unremarked part of educated speech.

My favourite, largely unsubstantiated, theory on the origins of RP is that when the Hanoverian dynasty began at the end of the seventeenth century, these monarchs of German descent could not pronounce the flat 'A' sound we hear now most notably in northern English accents. So words like the North American and Regional English-sounding path, bath and grass became paath, baath and graass. The accent at court adapted to this sound rapidly. Much later, British universities adopted this rounding of the vowels, desirous of sounding more like courtiers and, therefore, higher class and better educated. The distillation of accents and the delineation of class was set in motion. The Americans, early settlers from Plymouth at their core, hold many of the keys to that original accent. Ironically though, American actors occasionally think they need to modify their accents, making them sound more British, in order to sound legitimately Shakespearean. All this is theory, of course, but the proof of the pudding, as is so often the case in my art, is in the eating. Whenever I hear Shakespeare spoken in any accent – other than RP – he comes alive. The very sound of a specific, non-RP accent, encourages audiences to think they can understand it a lot easier than with a *posh* accent.

In the mid-twentieth century, the richness and variety of British voices risked being drowned out. As far back as 1946, BBC broadcaster Wilfred Pickles lamented this threat, as he noted that the BBC's quest for an homogenized, standardized accent, RP, was in danger of swamping our diversity of voices.

To further reinforce the point in favour of other accents, I should mention voice expert Patsy Rodenburg's take on all this. Patsy, who I had the great privilege to work with at the RSC the first time I was there, once pointed out to me that whilst meaning is conveyed through the consonants, emotion is carried by the vowels. If we hear the word 'war' in RP, for example, it carries the sense of the word, but contains little other information. However, if it is delivered in the closest approximation of Shakespeare's accent that we can be reasonably certain of, it sounds much more like 'waar', with a beautifully expressive elongation of the vowel. Instantly, a blood-curdling image comes rushing in on us. In a nutshell, RP, today estimated to be spoken by less than 2 per cent of the UK population, is not the only authentic accent to speak Shakespeare's line in, just another accent that can be used to convey Shakespeare's poetry and prose.

These thoughts are not the given orthodoxy of my art, however, and I could see how Greg might have felt that we should persuade the powers that be that it was a good idea to set the play in Africa in the first place, before challenging them with a *strange* accent. However, he bravely, perhaps reluctantly, agreed. I then became immediately unsure of myself and began to seriously wonder if I was, in fact, taking an unnecessary risk. But risk is where the art is, surely, and so I determined that I would plunge in head-first, when the final read-through of our symposium began that afternoon.

As a side note, I have to say that the previous day's discussion around which African accent might be used, was fascinating in its potential controversy amongst the performers present. I'd tried accents with Shakespeare from my very earliest performances and had learnt that the accent chosen should never be so strong as to obscure the natural rhythms of the verse. Having mastered an East African, specifically Tanzanian, accent at the Young Vic Theatre in 1988, I'd used it again in 2004, to play the role of Troilus in *Troilus and Cressida* for BBC Radio 4. The accent is lyrical and gentle, with consonants that are crisp and clear. Rhythmically, it mirrors well the iambic pentameter, the prevailing de *dum* de *dum* de *dum* de *dum* de *dum* rhythm, alternating feminine (weak) and masculine (strong) stressed syllables, so prevalent in Shakespeare's writing.

To *be* or *not* to *be* that *is* the *question* . . .

(*Ham* 3.1.55)

If *mu*sic *be* the *food* of *love* play *on* . . .

(*TN* 1.1.1)

But *soft* what *light* through *yon*der *win*dow *breaks* . . .

(*RJ* 2.2.2)

A mirror of our natural speech patterns.

I'm *going* *down* the *road* to *get* some *milk* . . .
Do *you* have *change* so I can *park* my *car* . . .
I *think* that's *all* the *samples* *that* you *need* . . .

However, the rehearsal room on that first morning of the symposium was full of actors of mainly West African descent. Amongst those not directly connected to that side of the continent many had a Caribbean heritage. The source of the majority of African people who had been taken as slaves and transported to the Caribbean islands was largely the west coast of Africa. And so, when I suggested on the first day after our Standard English read-through that if we did attempt an African accent we should avoid the heavily syllabic rhythms of West Africa, the atmosphere became a little tense. One of the actors present had emigrated from Zimbabwe in the early 1990s. His counter-suggestion, that because the actors were all black there was no need to embellish that fact with an added African accent, was a very compelling point. After all, we don't add a Danish accent to *Hamlet* when we come to perform that play. However, I persevered, offering my honest opinion that the richness of an African accent was vital to our exploration. I think I largely won Greg over. Those who thought I was being insulting to the origins of my parents' accent in leaning towards East Africa were mistaken. It felt right to avoid the, at times, heavy feel to some strongly syllabic accents, in such a subtle and passionate play. On top of this, I had recently heard that British actor Lenny Henry was shortly to star in Shakespeare's *Comedy of Errors* at the National Theatre and that he was set to use a Nigerian accent. That sounded great, because the rhyming scheme of that play would be enhanced by the almost staccato, syllabic sounds of West Africa that they had chosen. For our production of *Julius Caesar*, however, I felt it right to break this expectation and try a fresh accent for the audience. I'm not altogether sure whether I won that argument for all the actors present but I was going to give it a go on the final read-through, come what may. Shame neither Greg nor I thought to inform the other actors of my intent.

As the room settled down for the beginning of the read-through, you could sense a tightness that had not been present at any of the other sessions. It really wasn't a help either that Greg's partner, the skilful and ridiculously accomplished actor Sir Antony Sher, was also present. Not that he wasn't already on side, given his African roots and his personal attachments. Still, I was a bit daunted to be under his scrutiny.

The first scene is all about setting the context of the play and the actors playing Murellus and Flavius went to it with gusto; complete with their Standard English accents. That put the wind up me somewhat as I was still not 100 per cent confident about my earlier decision to try East African. Added to which, as stated earlier, none of the other actors had been apprised of my upcoming attempt. I honestly didn't want to put anybody off. However, Cassius and Brutus have a long duologue after Caesar, with the Senators, exits in the opening scene. I hoped that my first lines would give the actor playing Cassius, the same actor who had baulked at the idea of an accent in the first place, a clue as to how I was going to play it:

CASSIUS
    Will you go see the order of the course . . .?

BRUTUS
    Not I.

    Cassius insists.

CASSIUS
    I pray you do.

    And in full, to-hell-with-it, East African –

BRUTUS
    I am not gamesome.
    I do lack some part of that quick spirit
    That is in Antony . . .

In my peripheral vision, I could see that the actor reading Cassius had looked up. Whether he was scowling or just plain thrown, I could not tell. I finished the speech with my line:

BRUTUS
    Let me not hinder, Cassius, your desires.
    I'll leave you.

To his credit, 'Cassius' launched straight into an African accent that approximated mine and the whole room seemed to breathe a collective sigh of relief. We were off.

I didn't dare look at Greg as he's a nervous watcher at times, plus he had taken a big risk allowing me to attempt this accent, unheard by him. But the warmth of the African flavours that followed, despite the fact that they were variable in origin, gave the piece a life that I know we all felt was stronger than our previous read. We became more and more confident to explore the new-found sounds Shakespeare's words offered and the reading ended with an emotional flourish.

The end of the play is very moving, even in a dry reading, as the characters we've engaged in reach some understanding of who they are, shortly before they come to take their own lives. To my surprise, I wept, I hope not indulgently, as I felt there was a kind of happiness in Brutus on discovering how much he had been loved by all the men in his life, particularly the much-misunderstood Cassius. Antony Sher very kindly said that he much admired the almost joyful peace that impending death brought to Marcus Brutus. Truly gratifying. As was the hearty and lengthy applause that followed. It *could* work, and indeed we proved it *did* work in an African setting.

Journalist Yasmin Alibhai-Brown's adjudication during the post-read-through discussion was invaluable, as she lent her Kenyan history to the argument *for* this reading of *Julius Caesar*. In fact, the general tenor of the post-read-through forum from all quarters, including our three experts, Tom Holland, Richard Wilson and Martin Meredith was very positive. Greg – ably supported by a roomful of brilliant Shakespeareans – had managed to convince even the potentially sceptical that the RSC should explore the possibility of a full-scale production. We all went our separate ways knowing that we really could not have done any better.

Unsurprisingly, it was several months before the slow, grinding wheels of the monolith that is the RSC finally came to a decision and I was formally asked to take part in a production of *Julius Caesar* for the company. I gladly agreed. We were due to begin rehearsing in the early weeks of 2012.

8

The Roman Photo-Shoot

In February 2012, a short while before rehearsals began, I was asked to meet the other lead actors for a photo-shoot to promote the upcoming show. It always feels odd to be asked to be 'in character' for a photo, when you haven't even begun to explore in any detail who your character really is. For an actor, it's a bit like being asked to pretend to be in love with someone on camera having never met before that moment on set. Though, come to think of it, actors are asked to do that all too often. Our only solution was to give an approximation of the way our characters might stand and rely on Greg to say whether it suited the vague picture he had at that pre-rehearsal stage. The set for the photo-shoot was a mound of red-earth or half-globe. This would symbolize both the soil of Africa and the fact that it was the year of the World Shakespeare Festival.

Caesar, played by Jeffery Kissoon, would be atop the summit, centre, arm raised aloft; Marc Antony, Ray Fearon, close by but a little downhill, as it were. Brutus, me, and Cassius, played by Cyril Nri, would be together on the other side of Caesar, but on the same level as Antony, set in conspiratorial pose. Surreal, but necessary, as the fight for publicity in the theatre in the face of television and film presence is fierce. I was mildly irked that we had to prematurely expose our characters in this way but that seems to be part of the bargain you make when you venture into something so commercially dependent.

One could easily be forgiven for thinking that an outfit such as the RSC, that is subsidized by various bodies including the Arts Council, to the tune of several millions of pounds, would have no need to pander to the drive for publicity and attention-seeking that powers the film and television industries. However, if you consider the market we are in, it isn't so surprising. The entertainment market is saturated by big-budget movies with mega-stars and equally mega publicity budgets, so it is expedient, if not downright imperative, that theatrical productions make as big a noise as possible in order to generate the audience numbers sufficient enough to help pay the wages of a cast of twenty actors, not to mention a sizeable crew of technicians. It is all too easy to see why it was beneficial for the production to start the publicity ball rolling as soon as possible.

Having said all that though, I'd much rather not have stood in an African cloth or toga – a thing I'd never worn before – in a breezy, south-west London studio, on a freezing February evening, making a Brutus-face at Cyril Nri. I'd known Cyril as an acquaintance for many years but had never had the opportunity to work with him. He appeared to take the whole thing in his humorous stride and that made this awkward experience seem a little less alien.

Curiously, the hour or so we spent waiting for the photo to be taken was quite telling for the personalities revealed. Theatre and film director Sam Mendes has been quoted as saying that the skill of a director consists of 20 per cent direction and 80 per cent casting. I'd wholeheartedly agree with that. His casting of Shakespeare's *Troilus and Cressida* in 1990 for the RSC was nothing short of masterful: Troilus, Ralph Fiennes; Cressida, Amanda Root; Helen, Sally Dexter; Pandarus, Norman Rodway; Achilles, Cíaran Hinds: Thersites, Simon Russell Beale.

Well, how had Greg Doran fared with his casting of the essential roles in *Julius Caesar*? There was the rather giddy – over-friendly – greeting of all present, by me. I politely shook hands with, and introduced myself to, the photo-shoot crew who we'd probably never see again; there we see Brutus, making friends and influencing people. Then Cyril, giving forth about his recent exploits – a heart-on-his-sleeve Cassius if ever there was one. Jeffery, having seen it all and done it all, smiling patiently at the slow deliberations of the 'techies'; the leader of men, indulgent, but slightly impatient. Adjoa, also present, was calm poise personified; patient and tolerant to a fault, while observing *everything*. My perfect Portia. And finally, the star of the public show, Ray Fearon as Marc Antony, taking longer than any of us to get ready, due to a change of costume and a session in the make-up chair for a hair trim and general grooming. All of us, clearly, perfectly cast.

I left the studio that day a little more enlightened about the play and Greg's possible take on it. The positions on the *globe*, and the final casting decisions, had revealed much to me. I was greatly looking forward to being a part of the upcoming journey.

* * *

The first day of rehearsal was only a few weeks away when I started learning my lines for Brutus. This is something I've tended to avoid, except when I'm asked to by a director. Greg's reasoning was understandable. After only four weeks in the rehearsal room we would be filming *Julius Caesar* for the BBC's *Cultural Olympiad* season, which would include Shakespeare's history plays: *Richard II* with Ben Whishaw, *Henry IV Parts One & Two*, starring Jeremy Irons and *Henry V*, with Tom Hiddleston in the title role. Exalted company, indeed. But we would have a very short time to come up to the mark, plus our budget was going to be considerably less than those

FIGURE 1 *Poster of the 2012 RSC production of* Julius Caesar.
(Credit: RSC)

high-powered productions. If we couldn't film it in the fourteen days allotted to us we'd be stuffed. And so, learn my lines I did.

Cramming lines is not the easiest way to get them in. If one has the chance, a nice rehearsal-based method is best. You sit with the text around a table for a week, going through each scene, each line, practically each word and its meaning. You stand up and move, tentatively. Feeling your way around the space. In this way, you solidify the 'word with the action', as Hamlet tells the players. The lines tend to go in and stay in, as they are linked with intent, emotion and movement. Learning lines without another actor present, is harder, not to mention fraught with dangers. If you catch a nice phrasing that you enjoy, you can get stuck like a scratched record, only with great difficulty stopping yourself saying it like that all the time, regardless of counter suggestions from the director or subtle nuances from your fellow performer. If you can't change what you do when you play the scene with another actor, who may be offering you something unexpected, then you are not alive in that moment and exploration becomes stifled, if not impossible. Therefore, I had to tread a fine line between fixing the intent and tone while keeping it free enough so that I could change tack if my fellow actor gave me something else.

I suppose if you have worked with an actor many times before you can sort of second guess how they'll play it but that was not the case with either Cyril, playing Cassius, or Adjoa Andoh, Portia. And, to add a little more spice to the pot, the East African accent had to be simultaneously threaded into the learning process as this affects the rhythm tremendously. If one tries reading the same text in two very different accents one will immediately see what I mean. Accent is character and attitude and culture. Without it, we're bland and nondescript. It is the colour palette that transforms black and white words on a page into a recognizably living human being. So, before I finally plunged in to learning my lines, I had a Skype conversation with the brilliant dialect and accent coach, Penny Dyer.

I'd worked with Penny on my Incan accent for Peter Schaffer's *The Royal Hunt of the Sun* at the National Theatre in 2006. The accent was fiendishly difficult to place as we were dealing with a people who had been all but wiped out by their Spanish invaders, and the European diseases they'd carried with them. The modern Peruvian accent is a mixture of the accents found amongst the native South American populace and their Spanish colonists. It wasn't, therefore, possible to do anything other than approximate the accent our characters would have had pre-Pizarro and the Spanish invaders. Add to this, the fact that I was playing Atahualpa, King and God of the Incas – a man never to be gazed at except by his close inner circle and never touched by anyone, other than his wives – and you can see how ingenious Penny needed to be to find a unique, but comprehensible, accent for this unusual man. His interactions with others would have been very limited, so any accent would have been specific to him alone. These were people who lived rarefied lives at high altitudes, therefore their timbre would have sounded strange to Europeans.

There seemed to be in Atahualpa an innocence and trust, which may well have led to him being easily deceived by Pizarro and, unwittingly, to his people being overrun by the Spanish. His ultimate betrayal by Pizarro is one of those all too familiar tragedies of the Ancient World; a vast and powerful empire of great beauty and richness, meets European greed, ignorance and brutality, and suffers devastating, fatal damage in the process.

The voice Penny and I finally hit upon for Atahualpa was a cross between a Mandela-esque throatiness and a mild, almost Chinese, lightness. At least one critic felt the other-worldliness that I displayed in my accent and performance was merely camp. A shame, but I learnt then that you can't write a thesis for folks before the show starts, only hope they have the respect and trust to know that the background work has been done, the choices well-researched and justified.

Of course, it would be the same for Brutus. The accent used would indubitably divide audiences as we already saw in microcosm at the very first read-through. A Standard English rendition and some would wonder if we had felt an African accent would obscure Shakespeare's language. Others, that we had stripped Africa of its distinct flavour. If we went for a full-throttle West African it would be recognizable and, albeit clichéd, acceptable to many. Some would hate this, too, naturally, claiming it was not the way Shakespeare intended it to be heard. The fact that we had gone for a proto-Kenyan accent would mean a challenge for all; actors and the audience, unused for the most part to hearing those sounds. And, as in the Atahualpa case, you couldn't produce a sheet before the show to explain the choice, only hope that the majority of spectators accepted the decision and got on with enjoying the human interactions. That is, after all, the sole purpose of presenting plays; an attempt to show a slice of life; how human beings cope, or not, with the challenges the story throws up for them. Everything else we do is just a matter of framing and nuance; story – the human story – in the final analysis, is everything.

My first session with Penny Dyer on the ropey Skype connection was unusual but very useful. Much to my relief, we'd been thinking along reasonably similar lines since the symposium read-through, so she only had a few adjustments to make to bring my accent choice closer to her own. One of the things we needed to decide together was whether certain words should have RP or Kenyan endings. Suffixes like –ion, for example, could be heard on our various Kenyan voice samples to be pronounced either with a broad 'ee-on' sound, or with a more RP 'shun' sound. (Try: competition – compateesheeon/compateeshun.) It seemed to Penny and me that wherever the RP choice could legitimately be made, then this should be the one we would go for. Over the years, I've learnt that it doesn't make sense to be so authentic in your accent that you arrest the hearer's ear every time you say a particular word, especially, as in our case, if the Kenyan speakers we were listening to chose to alternate between both sounds. Over-meticulousness would only slow down comprehension for the listener. And that's the last thing you want with an auditorium half-packed with fear-paralysed spectators, for the most part told how difficult Shakespeare is from the time they were first introduced to him. We want them to relax after the first few speeches, fancying they have a chance of following all this. Maybe of even enjoying it. No small feat for any company who can manage that. Having made those foundational choices with Penny, I could now begin to slowly learn the lines for Brutus, making an educated guess as to what the final accent might sound like.

In my loft room at home, I began by looking at the first speeches from Act 1. In his first scene, Brutus is in no mood to speak to anyone, least of all Cassius, and his reluctance and reticence to talk give him a definite clipped, formal tone. This was immediately apparent, giving me an insight into his contained and controlled personality straight away.

CASSIUS
    Will you go see the order of the course?

BRUTUS
    Not I.

CASSIUS
    I pray you do.

BRUTUS
    I am not gamesome; I do lack some part
    Of that quick spirit that is in Antony.
    Let me not hinder, Cassius, your desires;
    I'll leave you.

                                                    (*JC* 1.2.25–31)

To repeat a phrase young actors hear all the time – 'if you're playing old, find where they are young, if you're playing young, find where they are old'. I'd always extrapolated from this idea that we are all contradictions of ourselves. Therefore, where there is stoicism, there is nearly always great passion; where there is meekness, there is, of necessity, great power. This, in a very small nutshell, is the source of much subtext and an essential component of the texture of character.

As I sat on the floor of the loft room with the early spring sun beaming down on me, I felt very aware of the privilege of having time to slowly, quietly, speak these words aloud. Of having the time for the thoughts to slot together smoothly. A throwback to my very first encounter with Shakespeare, you may recall. It occurred to me that I might like to always learn my lines this way for plays in the future. It allows you to solely focus on the logic of the text, because you're not having to negotiate your own nervousness in a rehearsal room – perhaps a little fearful of trying different ways of doing it.

And though I've said earlier that learning lines this way can lead to an overly fixed approach, it doesn't have to. In fact, I'm now convinced that the confidence I came into the rehearsal room with on the first day, was due, in large part, to this slow and relaxed working-through of thought with text; the logic of one scene and mood following another. The other great insight that occurred to me in going through the play in this way, was just how changeable Brutus is, not just from act to act but from scene to scene and even within one scene.

Take, for example, Act 2 Scene 1, set in the orchard or garden of Brutus' home. He starts the scene alone, desperately trying to make sense of the murderous course he's all but decided on. By the end of his monologue he is convinced that Caesar's death is justified. Then comes the boy Lucius, and Brutus is a slightly fractious employer. After Lucius leaves, Brutus has to deal with the fiery indignation that has risen in him, provoked by the note thrown through his window from a mystery citizen, daring to question his brave ancestry. Again, when a knock comes at the gate and he peremptorily dismisses his servant, he is revealed as a man still at war with the actions he is close to taking. But then, with the entrance of the conspirators, we see the commander of men, able to convince the gathered conspirators of his right to lead them. When they leave, after he has roused them all to noble action, he speaks tenderly to his sleeping servant and here we glimpse his gentler side. This is followed by a deeply vulnerable exposure of the man in his conversation with his wife, Portia, and a near-breakdown, before pulling himself together to once again show us the leader of men in conversation with the frail old man Caius Ligarius. And that's just his second scene.

I decided, after learning that scene, that I needed to play Brutus moment by moment. Not think ahead too much as to what it meant to act this way or that but to be reactive to each separate event. I thought that, far from making him schizophrenic in some way or just plain incomprehensible as a character, it would give me a multi-faceted view of him and show him to be the creation Shakespeare wanted him to be. A man, like us, full of contradictions and struggles; a man at once sure and insecure, brave and frightened, in short, a rounded human being and, arguably, one of the first truly psychologically complex, non-fictional characters Shakespeare crafted. That prince of mutability, Hamlet, was to follow only a few years after this play. Shakespeare was honing his craft in *Julius Caesar* and his complexity of plot, character and inner life was intensified here.

With my lines finally *in*, after a fortnight of daily cramming sessions, I prepared for rehearsals to start. But what I hadn't guessed was that it would not be a rehearsal period that resembled anything I'd been through before. I was about to be reminded that, in this art, you never finish learning.

9

Rehearsals

On a sunny day in March, I walked out of Clapham North tube station on my way to the RSC rehearsal rooms, for my first day on *Julius Caesar*. It seemed like an odd place to have come back to after a twenty-year absence. I can't pretend there wasn't a part of me wondering if I'd remember all too soon precisely why I hadn't been back since 1992.

As detailed in Chapter Three, my first and last stint with the RSC began in 1990 and ended in relief and near exhaustion, two years later. In that intensely isolated period of my life, the one saving grace was the work and I'm enormously grateful that it was so fulfilling. All of the productions I participated in had given me great insights into Shakespeare's work and, indeed, myself. It helped shape the choices and thrust of my career ever since. What I learnt back then I used in 2004 when I directed *Romeo and Juliet* with amateurs from Harlesden, my old neck-of-the-woods. Our production, which was presented at RADA's Jerwood Vanbrugh Theatre, was filmed for Channel 4 for a documentary called *My Shakespeare*. My confidence that even kids who claimed to have no opinion on Shakespeare would eventually catch fire when presented with an opportunity to perform one of his plays, was fully justified. These first-timers, sourced from the streets of north-west London and ranging from seventeen to fifty-two, were absolutely brilliant. I'm moved by their performances every time I watch that film.

However, a cloud of faintly negative memories hung persistently over my head despite the sunshine, as I climbed the steps of the rehearsal venue on the appropriately named Cato Road. (The aforementioned Cato: Portia's father.) Would the length of this job, like my first boot-camp stint at the RSC, end in theatre-fatigue? Flying in the face of those thoughts, I decided that it was time to change my attitude and let today be a new start in my history with the RSC.

The first thing of note, in contrast with the last time I was in the building, was just how clean, light and airy it felt in the green room. And the warmth of the welcome brought back that feeling of optimism and excitement at the end of the symposium, all those months ago. I met several of the cast who had been at that first reading and noticed many new, and keen, faces. I was very happy to see that Simon Manyonda had agreed to play Lucius, Brutus' servant. I'd admired Simon's acting ever since seeing him in *Welcome* to *Thebes* at the National Theatre. And, meeting him a little while after that production, I found him an articulate and talented young performer. It was vital that I had an actor that I trusted in the role of Lucius, as he would potentially be the most important character for my Brutus. After all, it is with Lucius that Brutus expresses himself more honestly than with anybody else in the play. It is Lucius, too, who, in Greg's production at least, will agree to take Brutus' life when everyone else has deserted him. Strato, the obscure character Shakespeare has performing this dreadful task, was cut, giving Simon the opportunity to plot Lucius' narcolepsy as a theme that was threaded throughout the play. It also meant that the boy-servant would become the boy-soldier, jolted awake at the end of the play in order to take the life of his master. A great innovation of Greg's and handled with masterful ease by Simon. Manyonda claims that I had whispered the narcolepsy thread to him during a read-through. I doubt his account, but I'm happy to take the credit for this clever piece of character plotting.

Cyril, Ray and Jeffery were all present, of course. Adjoa and I were happy to be finally starting the process for real. Greg was relaxed and chatty, the atmosphere bubbly and buzzing. We had recently learnt that Greg was to take over as artistic director of the RSC, so the excitement of starting a whole new era was in the air. We were all invited to grab drinks – and one more biscuit – and make our way to the rehearsal room on the next floor up, to start day one.

Michael Boyd, the outgoing artistic director, gave us a rundown of just how unique this production was already. It would be the first time a company of RSC actors would consist solely of black performers and, if the recent rumours of a potential visit to the Moscow Art Theatre came true, the first RSC company to perform in Russia since 1968.

Deborah Shaw, head of the World Shakespeare Festival, roused us with the thought that we were in the vanguard of what the largest, oldest and most prestigious British Shakespeare company would be offering in the London Olympic year of 2012. The World Shakespeare Festival would be an ambitious and unprecedented collaboration between the UK's leading arts institutions. It would form a major part of the Cultural Olympiad; bringing together leading artists from all over the world, in a UK-wide festival. A celebration of the works of Shakespeare that would include the likes of the British Museum, Tate Modern, the National Theatre and, with its international reach, Shakespeare's Globe and their Globe to Globe Festival. Participants from all over the world would be involved in staging Shakespeare's works in many different languages and in a myriad of diverse forms. The online presence of this exciting project – running from April 2012 to November 2014 – would touch hundreds of schools and thousands of pupils worldwide. Countries involved included Oman, India, Brazil, Czech Republic, Hong Kong, the USA and South Africa. Being even a small part of this unique project was very humbling indeed.

While it could have felt like a daunting task, those of us fortunate enough to have been part of it had a confidence instilled in us by the symposium. It meant that the core group of actors avoided any potentially choking nerves. On top of that, Niamh O'Flaherty, Deborah's assistant, was so excited by the prospects for the play that we felt like we'd triumphed before we'd even started.

The other members of the ensemble were the sterling stage managers, led by our great company manager, Ben Tyreman. His team included Patricia Davenport, deputy stage manager, who'd be in rehearsals every day, making copious notes on our props and moves and generally keeping a clearly boisterous group of actors in check. She possesses not only the most amazing ginger Afro but also has the gift of an absolute foghorn of a voice. Wisdom swiftly dictated that one avoided being next to her when she was calling us all to order. There was Suzanne Bourke, our stage manager – efficiency personified with a touch of genuine care, the perfect combination for that role. And helping her and pretty much everyone else was our assistant stage manager, Jo Vimpay – quietly brilliant at everything. Our movement was to be undertaken by Struan Leslie, an expert on physicality, who would prove to be essential in getting us all to embed ourselves in a less Western mode of being. Our choreographer was Diane Mitchell, busy across town taking the Olympic opening ceremony performers through their paces. She'd be responsible for drilling the British actors tasked with trying to convince us that they were born-and-bred African dancers. She did far more than help us to avoid embarrassment, however. Her choreography at the start of the show was electrifying, not just for the audience but also for the actors in the wings. It helped root us in the continent and atmosphere of Africa itself.

Lyn Darnley was to be the most useful and essential part of the creative team for me. Her work on my voice ensured that I kept my full vocal range for eight gruelling months – a first in my career.

Quite a team.

* * *

Greg launched the rehearsal process with a game, consisting of us all stating three facts about ourselves. It was one of those exercises that can cause some embarrassment and lead to all sorts of revelations about our fellow actors. For instance, amongst the martial arts nuts, tennis fans and amateur musicians in the group, we had Cyril Nri, claiming to have been hired only because he'd once slept with Greg and also that he happened to be of German descent. All untrue, I hasten to add. A hint at his eccentricity and sense of fun. Despite Cyril's joshing, the game did its job and broke the ice. It also gave us an initial snapshot view of the group as a whole.

This rather irreverent, jokey persona of Cyril's belied the deep-thinking man beneath. He told me later how important this play was to him. Twenty years before, he had dreamt of doing a version of *Julius Caesar*, performing and setting it in the Nigerian region formerly known as Biafra. He had fled the Biafran War, also known as the Nigerian Civil War, as an infant. In Cyril's version of the play, that devastating conflagration, super-imposed on *Julius Caesar*, would be partly seen as incited by the 'sibling' rivalry between General Yakubu Gowon and General Emeka Ojukwu (both educated in the UK, at Oxford University and Sandhurst Military Academy, respectively). Thanks to Cyril, the subject of sibling sentiment fuelling bitter conflict bled into our show, as we will see. His hope for this production was that, despite having a white, middle-class director at the helm, we would avoid what he described as 'The Disneyfication of Africa' by white, and indeed, some African-American directors.

He needn't have worried. Greg was incredibly aware of the position he was in. His respect for the actors of African descent, whose knowledge of that continent was far superior to his own, was clear from the start. No one could have felt patronized in the least. Cyril wasn't the only actor who needed assurance that we were not going to be exploited as an exotic African safari production for the RSC. We were all aware of how easily this could have been the case despite the best will in the world. Wisely, Greg took much of his lead from the actors in the room and with Tayo Akinbode in charge of music and Diane Mitchell overseeing our choreography, we were in very safe and knowledgeable hands. As Samantha Lawson, who was understudying the role of Calphurnia, Caesar's wife, has pointed out to me, the atmosphere that Greg created immediately relaxed us all. Even those amongst us who had little experience of Shakespeare were never made to feel we had no voice in the room. A deftly humble method of getting us all on side from Greg, here.

* * *

Our first text-based work was investigating the idea of rhetoric as a three-pronged attack. *Ethos*, the laying out of the personal world view; *Pathos*, the emotional appeal; and finally *Logos*, logic and the right words. For this, we were given an extract from one of Shakespeare's other Roman plays, *Titus Andronicus*, and a scene in which the two sons of the recently deceased Emperor try to win the citizens' affections in order to inherit the throne. Saturninus is in warring mood, but his brother Bassianus utilizes more dignified tones to evoke the ancient spirit of the True Roman.

Ray took the first speech and I was given the follow-up. It was indicative of how Greg saw the two methods of crowd control in the post-assassination Forum Scene that he had us, so early on, demonstrating the different approaches in rhetorical speech. Saturninus, with all the indignation of the robbed first-born, appeals to the lowest form of mob energy – violence. Bassianus, in contrast, is content to let the citizens decide the question of who rules them, in an orderly and dignified manner. Shakespeare's first tragedy gives us two contrasting methods of winning friends and influencing people.

SATURNINUS

> Noble patricians, patrons of my right,
> Defend the justice of my cause with arms.
> And, countrymen, my loving followers,
> Plead my successive title with your swords.
> I am his first born son that was the last
> That ware the imperial diadem of Rome.
> Then let my father's honours live in me,
> Nor wrong mine age with this indignity.

BASSIANUS

> Romans, friends, followers, favourers of my right,
> If ever Bassianus, Caesar's son,
> Were gracious in the eyes of royal Rome,
> Keep then this passage to the Capitol
> And suffer not dishonour to approach
> The imperial seat, to virtue consecrate,
> To justice, continence, and nobility,
> But let desert in pure election shine
> And, Romans, fight for freedom in your choice.

> > (*Tit* 1.1.1–17)

This speech does not mean that Bassianus is against war of any kind, but is trying to appeal to a higher nature in the citizenry; Brutus' mistake, too, some might say. Amongst the cast, it was hard to find anyone who didn't think it was obvious that Brutus was wrong to appeal to the crowd's higher instincts. They felt, for the most part, that his idealism was misplaced and naïve. Killing Antony alongside Caesar also seemed a no-brainer solution. In fact, Brutus preventing the other conspirators killing Antony was seen as the chief problem of the play; namely, that the conspiracy is undermined by the living embodiment of revenge, Antony. If Brutus had merely put aside his noble desire to be in the right – the argument goes – and had killed Antony, along with his best friend Caesar, the conspiracy would have carried the day and we'd no longer be discussing the rights and wrongs of Brutus' choices.

I find this view very disturbing for a number of reasons. The first is that it assumes the intrinsic point of political rebellion is the taking of absolute power by any means necessary. 'You can't make an omelette without breaking moral eggs', might be the mantra of the proponents of this particular philosophical tenet. However, it shows a distinctly negative bias of aspiration within mankind, that we would consider that the most important aspect of any revolution is the taking of power. Surely, in order to truly win the hearts and minds of people to a cause, it is essential to show that the motivations of the chief protagonists are empty of selfish ambition. Mandela? Martin Luther King? I believe we'd ideally want our potential leaders to have a disinterested desire to see their people free – more specifically, free to choose their leaders. The alternative is a state of fear. Such a state destroys with impunity those who oppose the primary revolution. Russian and French revolutions had this in common; after the initial pogroms there followed a sustained campaign of terror and fear, against both actual and suspected enemies. Friends soon turned into foes, those not in favour were tainted with the stain of counter-revolution and subsequently persecuted, many to the point of death. Is this really the political solution that we consider makes the most sense?

The second point that disturbs me is related. When we talk of nobility, justice and honour as weaknesses, it exposes our negatively skewed morality. It isn't just that these qualities are objectively good; they are essential for empathy. And empathy, that most undervalued of human qualities, is what should motivate anyone seeking political office and influence. Caring about your fellow citizens, putting yourself in their shoes and holding their rights as sacred as your own should be a prerequisite for high office. But if these are not valued, then the only thing that really counts is the simple ability to wield power over others. Julius Nyerere, one of the first African leaders who voluntarily stepped down from high office, is the perfect example of this benevolently gracious letting go.

My further concern is that if the next generation of artists isn't aware of, or worse actively disrespects, the highest aspirations that their fellow men and women can attain to, then what hope is there for our pragmatic politicians? We can't hold one set of people accountable for a lack of the same moral underpinning that *we* suffer from. Art, the arts, should rise above the status quo, showing us visions of a better way; a way of connection, not its opposite. Not didactically, but as an offering, not for answers but, at the very least, posing the questions; showing us alternatives to the route of power-grabbing at all costs.

The two speeches of Bassianus and Saturninus show us immediately the clarity and power of rhetoric at its best. Pathos, revealing who we are emotionally; ethos, exposing the foundations of our world view; and finally logos, a detailed setting out of the logic of our argument, all brilliantly contained in a few lines of public speaking with the brothers verbally fencing before the fickle populace. Shakespeare, near his prime in *Julius Caesar*, was to give full bent to those skills established in this play in the works that quickly followed: *As You Like It*, *Twelfth Night* and the pinnacle of his achievements in the year 1600, *Hamlet*.

* * *

Usually, a rehearsal process is roughly divided into two sections: sitting down, reading and discussing the play, followed by getting up and physicalizing our findings from the first sessions. But here is where the process began to surprise and delight me. Though, it must be said, I was also guilty of a little frustration, too. It wasn't going as I'd presumed. My first bone of contention came in the first read-through. Normally, this consists of actors reading their roles tentatively. We might break off now and then to discuss a line that doesn't quite make sense or a dialogue cut that makes comprehension a little difficult. In these cases, we would, ordinarily, look back over the unedited text, deciding if we shouldn't reinstate excised lines. My favourite part of this exercise is discussing and justifying the actions and words of my character. As I have said earlier, I'd dissected much of what was motivating Brutus and felt that I had a clear line to his pattern of thinking and, subsequently, the choices this then led to. This was going to be relatively easy, fun even. But that was not Greg's method here. Instead of allowing us all to pontificate on our individual character's inner lives, he suggested that each character in each scene was to be read by an actor *not* playing that role. In effect, I felt he had put a gagging order on the individual actor and this I found very hard to deal with. In fact, at one point, when something particularly outrageous and clearly, to me, wrong was said about Brutus' motivation in a given scene, I had to leave the room for five minutes or risk blurting out my thoughts and ruining the exercise.

I have now come to think that Greg's madness had a great deal of method in it. Silencing the insider knowledge of the actor who had studied the role, and who'd gone a long way to imagining how it would be played, had two extremely positive effects. The first, it pinpointed areas of fixed attitudes in that mute actor towards their character. The second, it allowed the way other people see the character to be exposed, before the person playing them had had a chance to fully lock down their approach. Imagine if all your friends – as well as perfect strangers – were allowed to comment on your personality and choices but you were unable to reply or contradict. Frustrating, no doubt, but priceless in delineating the dichotomy between a character's desired effect on their world and their actual impact in that world.

Speaking to Greg some time after these sessions, he exposed a third, far from negligible, benefit. Those actors who have, in the final analysis, very few words in the piece can be made very early on to feel peripheral to the life of the play. As they hear the same four or five actors taking the lion's share of the text, it can lead to feelings of disconnection, potentially harming that actor's ability to fully commit to the telling of the story. All in all, it worked very well and, apart from four or five occasions where I had to bite my tongue, I think I coped well with it.

Cyril had even more trouble than me in separating his personal view of Cassius and the obvious criticisms that can be aimed at such a complex character. Perhaps his early decision to paint Cassius as a classic manic depressive – with his violent mood swings, disproportionate loyalties and suicide threats – helped to make him feel responsible for this character in a very personal way. To varying degrees, I think the same could be said for all of us. Eventually, however, I felt it was important to try to keep a little distance between what I thought empathetically of Brutus as *my* character and his own actions as judged by others.

* * *

I clowned around a lot in that first week or two. I don't know if that was a manifestation of nerves at the task ahead and the lack of time to complete it or if it was just a mild hysteria brought on by the thought of how long this job was going to go on for. I'd left home on the weekend and would not be returning for about three weeks. My wife and I had always said that three weeks is about the acceptable length of separation. My son, eight at the time, was beginning to grow intolerant of time apart from me, too. It wasn't going to be easy for any of us. I function better when I'm at home or able to go home regularly, so the thought of the upcoming time away was a possible factor in my slight hyperactivity. March till, roughly speaking, October, suddenly began to feel like a long eight months.

10

The Stage of Enlightenment

After the initial terror of standing up, exposed, and walking and talking as the character, an actor begins to grow in confidence. Actors are a tentative bunch at times. And the confidence-trick of representing a Shakespearean character is one of the most testing games of nerve. Why would that be? For me, the obvious answer is the weight of history, theatrical and, in this case, literally historical, that bears down on you when you dare to strut about the stage declaring yourself a Brutus, Caesar or Portia. The desire not to mess it up is strong. Most actors won't take on these challenges lightly.

But, as was said to me many years before when I played Bill Sykes at primary school, I was the only actor playing that role at that particular moment. I should be proud to hold that responsibility and carry it with confidence. (The truth is probably more prosaic than that and there are about fifty 'Bruti' strutting their stuff at any one time on the planet.) Nevertheless, the feeling of being responsible for a character is a strong and, potentially, nerve-shredding one. My trick to avoid being rendered rigid with the fear that I am inadequate to represent great men? I immediately latch on to aspects of my character that ring true as recognizable, human-sized behaviour. I relish the sense of filling out the gaps a playwright, even one as excellent as Shakespeare, has left in a character's humanity. Take the several snappy exchanges Brutus has with his servant Lucius in the Orchard Scene.

BRUTUS
What, Lucius, ho! . . .
Lucius, I say!
I would it were my fault to sleep so soundly.
When, Lucius, when? Awake, I say! What, Lucius!

And later . . .

. . . Get you to bed again, it is not day.
Is not tomorrow, boy, the ides of March?

LUCIUS
I know not, sir.

BRUTUS
Look in the calendar, and bring me word.

LUCIUS
I will, sir.

(JC 1.3.1–43)

Simon's Lucius was rather disgruntled and teenaged in his manner, always half-asleep, bothered. But the rather dry dialogue between the two left something to be desired, so Simon and I developed a father–son feeling between us as characters. The son, Lucius, being as described above and the father, Brutus, a demanding and forceful parent. The rounded, human touch we were then able to bring to this relationship was highlighted by the short speech that followed the tense scene with the conspirators, ultimately leading Brutus into the more open-hearted conversation with Portia. Brutus finds his servant asleep, again, but instead of admonishing him, we hit upon a softer take. Brutus strokes the head of his oblivious, sleeping servant, and quietly whispers, almost to himself:

BRUTUS
. . . It is no matter,
Enjoy the honey-heavy dew of slumber.
Thou hast no figures nor no fantasies,
Which busy care draws in the brains of men;
Therefore, thou sleep'st so sound.

(JC 2.1.228–32)

It was one of those moments in rehearsal that is bred of two people sharing an empty stage, as Brook might have it. On the page, it is merely a functional relationship; Brutus must have a servant to bring him the note thrown in at the window. But, once the two men are onstage together, their attitudes toward one another become the more interesting part of their relationship. I love these accidental moments of enlightenment that spring from the justification of scripted action that live theatre brings.

One other example from the same scene is the moment when Portia corners Brutus, forcing him to confront his lack of self-disclosure. In the theatre, one actor does not need to face another for the audience to know that they are having an intimate exchange. In fact, when one actor has a speech that seeks to penetrate the other character, it is very effective if that other character faces away from them and out to the watching audience. This might seem counter-intuitive and may not always work on camera, for example. But onstage, it is like a close-up for the audience as they get to see the effect the words are having on the character receiving them. Adjoa and I tried many ways to play this scene:

face to face, moving constantly, an improvised mix of both. But what we came to realize was that Portia had to be made to try very hard to get Brutus to *face* the truth and open his heart to her. The sheer volume of words demanded there be a journey of breaking him down; gradually revealing her stoical desperation.

PORTIA

> Is Brutus sick? And is it physical
> To walk unbracéd and suck up the humours
> Of the dank morning? What, is Brutus sick?
> And will he steal out of his wholesome bed
> To dare the vile contagion of the night,
> And tempt the rheumy and unpurgéd air
> To add unto his sickness?

(*JC* 2.1.260–6)

These questions were too direct for me to face it out with her. I needed to turn away, or risk lying to her face . . .

No, my Brutus,
You have some sick offense within your mind,
Which, by the right and virtue of my place,
I ought to know of; and upon my knees
I charm you, by my once commended beauty,
By all your vows of love, and that great vow
Which did incorporate and make us one,
That you unfold to me, yourself, your half,
Why you are heavy and what men tonight
Have had resort to you; for here have been
Some six or seven, who did hide their faces
Even from darkness.

(*JC* 2.1.266–77)

*And now he **has** to look at her to **justify** the next line.*

BRUTUS

> Kneel not, gentle Portia.

PORTIA

> I should not need, if you were gentle Brutus.

(*JC* 2.1.277–8)

This is a practical demonstration of what we mean when we say that Shakespeare writes stage directions for the actor within the spoken text. Now Portia has his attention, she can drive her point home with agonizing vulnerability. She wins his trust and the couple part, at peace with one another . . .

Adjoa and I knew then that we had the essence of their relationship. Honesty. Listening with respect. Intelligence naturally blended with tender love. These moments of discovery were foundational for the rest of the rehearsal process and deepened as the audience reaction showed us that they recognized this beautiful partnership of equals. Hints of this depth of relationship can be detected in the text but the full picture could only be seen when one performer looked another in the eye or, indeed, could not. I was fortunate in Adjoa that she teaches Shakespeare to young people, so her knowledge and insight is immense. Take her views on the way young women often approach Shakespearean roles. She finds that when she sits on an audition panel at a well-known drama school, the girls tend to use a haranguing tone when addressing male characters in their speeches. This, she rightly argues, is a diminution of a Shakespearean character's complexity and a reductive take on women in general. These roles are brilliant because they are as complex as any male role in the plays. Take a character like Margaret from the History Plays, for example. She begins as a young woman and ends as a matriarch, seasoned by sorrow, who has buried practically all the men she's ever loved in her life. Adjoa concluded that Shakespeare knew full well how women had to negotiate their way in a largely male-led world and he was far too sensitive and empathetic to reduce them to scolds or nags. It was largely Adjoa's intelligent, rooted and fleshed-out interpretation of Portia that gave our onstage relationship such power, weight and truth.

The beauty of Shakespeare is that he loves to throw domestic drama into the midst of the historic. It's why we still recognize these characters after two-thousand years of history has gone by. Not by their actions alone but by their humanity as expressed in Shakespeare's simple, poetic genius.

We were regularly treated to the sight of our fellow actors finding gems in this early rehearsal period. A tribute to the liberty and safety of the environment Greg was instrumental in nurturing. Watching Ray Fearon the first time he played, off-book, the speech over Caesar's dead body, was an electrifying and memorable moment.

ANTONY
Oh, pardon me, thou bleeding piece of earth,
That I am meek and gentle with these butchers . . .

(*JC* 3.1.254–5)

Joe Mydell's masterful take on Casca was another revelation; a character that starts so vibrantly and cynically who Shakespeare rather lets down, in my opinion. But Joe made the most of this sharp, silver-tongued showman:

CASSIUS
Did Cicero say any thing?

CASCA
Ay, he spoke Greek.

CASSIUS
  To what effect?

CASCA
  Nay and I tell you that, I'll ne'er look you in the face again. But those
  that understood him smiled at one another and shook their heads;
  but, for mine own part, it was Greek to me.

                                                    (*JC* 1.2.277–83)

Around this time, Cyril revealed his discovery that Cassius displayed some
of the classic symptoms of manic depression. In extreme cases this can lead
a person into developing strong attachments to people. If the 'other' lets
them down, betrays them in any way, the reaction is disproportionate to
the offence. What was a great love becomes, instantly, an intense hatred.
His relationship with Caesar, related to us in the first scene with Brutus,
being a case in point. A kind of blindness to the faults of the loved 'other'
can also be a part of this condition. For Cyril, it helped to know this,
as Cassius, a brilliant military strategist, constantly ceded to Brutus'
plans, even though he knew them to be wrong. A clever reading of the
character that allowed him to get through those scenes that have
thrown many a Cassius before him, desperate to find a logic to his illogical
decisions.
  Many great insights came in the first three weeks or so, not least of which
was the dawning realization that Cyril and I would have the monumental
task of holding the emotional line throughout the piece. It could be no other
way, we quickly saw, as scene after scene featured the two close friends in
either conspiratorial conversation or violent and vocal disagreement. The
Tent Scene argument was a powerful example of this.
  Initially, no matter how we tried to fathom the logic of the argument
surrounding the initial basis of their dispute – the mysterious character
Lucius Pella (never seen) and the bribe he took (or did not take) from the
Sardians – we could find little to ignite our passion. Greg, Cyril and I soon
realized that if this argument was going to interest the audience and if it was
Shakespeare's intent that it be important, then we would have to make the
argument about something much more personal: betrayal. Not just betrayal
of the cause, but the betrayal of one sibling by another. When, on a tired,
grey afternoon, we launched into the scene for the final time that day,
something extraordinary happened. We both reverted to children. Not just
men who were arguing in a childish way. Actual children who felt passionately
about their own righteous wounds in that profound way that only children
can. We roared, yes, but we also wept, pouted and despaired of ever being
understood by the one person who had always understood us. It was a
momentous, game-changing, leap into the heart of the play, into our
characters. In fact, that afternoon we realized that we had hit on something
not many productions had. The love of Brutus and Cassius, children of the

Republic, of course, but love between two children of the same blood, too. A powerfully unique and intimate moment in the whole *Julius Caesar* journey.

* * *

We had all started to embed our characters and could feel that vague sense of order that comes upon a company when they get over their initial tentativeness with one another. Though it was a large cast, there seemed to be a homogeny to the group very early on. Could this be due to the fact that we were an exclusively black cast?

My first experience of a black cast was in my second job after completing my training at LAMDA. It was at the Young Vic Theatre in London and I was performing in a play by David Holman called *Solomon and The Big Cat*; directed by its then artistic director, David Thacker. I played Solomon Mkonazi, an eleven-year-old Tanzanian boy who has found a mother and baby leopard, prompting him to solicit the help of the local ranger to save them from the poachers. Amongst the great cast was Pamela Nomvette, a brilliant Zimbabwe-born actor. She effortlessly played various roles.

Pamela was vociferous about the fact that not enough work was being given to non-white actors. She felt, too, that the roles offered generally veered towards the *exotic* or *ethnic*. She wondered what this word *ethnic* even meant in light of the fact that so many black, British-born artists were on the scene. She felt the institution of British theatre was stifling to black creative talent and that there was a defined glass-ceiling weighing against the rise of black talent.

I was a little thrown. I had not dwelt on this negative aspect of the theatrical world since I first decided to apply for drama training. My sister Pam, when I suggested that I might apply for drama school at the age of seventeen, had questioned my choice of career: 'Why would you want to do that, Pat? You'll only end up playing slaves and servants!' I suspect, in some ways, what I've been doing ever since is attempting to prove her wrong. In fact, at that time, I made a conscious effort to resist feeling second class and actively behaved as if the world were my oyster. Just in case any readers believe that this was an old attitude about casting, from way back in the 1980s, I spoke very recently to Samantha Lawson, who took over as Calphurnia for part of our tour. She recalled being told by young, white peers that she should not really be playing a Scandinavian witch in Philip Pullman's *His Dark Materials* as she was black. Unless, of course, they were doing a 'thing' where all the witches would be black. 'Juliet' was also out-of-bounds for Samantha, according to these same contemporaries of hers. A young actor friend had been complimented in her first season at the RSC by an older, white actor noting that she must be 'very good, indeed, to be a black actress at the RSC.' These attitudes are not dead, sadly, just shallowly buried at times.

My encouraging director at the Cockpit, who had spoken so articulately on the subject of writers creating multi-ethnic characters in their work, came back to me then. Experience has led me to modify my views somewhat since my youth theatre days. I feel that those writers have either not emerged in any great number or, more likely, they have not been urged strongly enough to write for a diverse audience and cast. On the grounds, perhaps, that the art of theatre in Britain is more business than art and, therefore, you could argue, must pay its way by appealing to an audience of paying, white people. This is false, detracts from the creative process and stymies the advancement of a multi-ethnic, multicultural artistic expression in the UK. Having lived on the continent in the past, I'd argue that that goes for much of the rest of European theatre, too.

Furthermore, I believe that there *is* a glass-ceiling but it is vaguer than my sister, or Pamela Nomvette, could have articulated at the time. Some truths can be stated, however. We live in a majority white country with a majority white literary tradition on television and in the theatre. That's a given. But that fact need not exclude actors who are not white from full participation in the arts. In recent years, various steps have been made to redress a real imbalance in the representation of people who are not white in our society. But we still have a long way to go till we reach the dizzy heights of a plethora of major black performers in our home-grown, mainstream theatre, television and films.

The cry from some producers – that ethnic minority actors can only draw a niche audience – is flying in the face of the facts. Great African American stars who can command major theatre and film roles in successful international projects, are not uncommon. Will Smith, Denzel Washington, Morgan Freeman, Halle Berry, Samuel L. Jackson, Viola Davis and Jamie Foxx to name a very few. We, on this side of the Atlantic, are confined by our much smaller industry, it's true, and a few black actors – and many more white ones – have found that success in the US they felt eluded them here. But, smallness need not be equated with exclusivity. Access should be available to all ethnicities, regardless of the demographics of population or of financial clout. But, if Oscar-nominated Chewetel Ijiofor and Sophie Okenedo, alongside David Harewood, Marianne Jean-Baptiste, David Oyelowo and the very successful Idris Elba, state that they have had to leave these shores to seek their fortunes, then something must be awry in our distribution of roles to excellent, leading black actors. The interesting thing to note about these names, by the way, is their obvious willingness to work here. Clearly, an often-frustrated desire as things stand.

It has taken me some time to reconcile Pamela's strong views with my own attitude of positive thinking, but I think I'm just about there. The world is not a fair place and the acting world even less so. So much depends, for all of us – regardless of ethnicity – on timing, height, weight, skin tone and a host of other near imponderables. It is impossible to guess which actor will get a certain role in a round of auditions because neither the director's nor the producer's whims can be quantified. The goal is to be excellent and trust that your skill will make room for you despite some of the disadvantages arising from the way you are perceived by the outside world. Surely this is a lesson for life in general, not just our rather irrational profession.

The thought of working with another black cast on the RSC's *Julius Caesar* intrigued me greatly. Would it make any difference? Would I, in fact, feel empowered? The truth is, it makes an immediate difference when every member of the cast has a similar take on life to yours by dint of the colour of their skin. This might sound counter-intuitive and a gross generalization and, in a way, it is both those things. How do we find a connection between a young woman brought up in the Cotswolds, to a Ghanaian father and a white, English mother who had to endure name-calling and taunts from her white contemporaries for most of her youth, with a Yorkshire lass who is bold, strong and exceedingly northern? How can a boy born and raised in Willesden Green in the 1960s and 1970s with St Lucian parents, be similar to a man born and raised in Savannah, Georgia in the 1950s? The answer is: easily. We all have one thing in common – the outside world perceives us as black before it perceives us as people. And that simple truth unites us like no other factor.

The next time I had the privilege to work with an exclusively black cast was in the 2003 production of Kwame Kwei-Armah's *Elmina's Kitchen* at the National Theatre. I played the role of Deli, a man trying desperately to keep his late mother's Caribbean restaurant (the 'Elmina' of the title) a going concern. In the face of the problem of his son desiring to follow the ways of the local gangster, Digger, and on top of his estrangement from his wayward father, Deli attempts to forge a life in the harsh environment he finds himself in. The tragic murder at the end of the play was harrowing to perform and powerful in its impact. The audience, wonderfully mixed for the most part, were moved and angered by it in turn. Seeing the faces of young people offering us a standing ovation, feeling their sense of affirmation at watching part of their lives represented onstage, will stay with me for the rest of my life. Has the momentum of that show abated? I think it has to a certain extent. The more experienced actors in the cast – George Harris, Dona Croll and Oscar James – had seen it all before and were realistic while still trying to remain positive. The glass ceiling, they said, was neither gone nor acknowledged; it had merely been placed a little higher.

One blogger, in response to an article I wrote in the *Guardian* newspaper, said that black performers should wake up to the fact that we are a minority and that we'll never get more than scraps from the white establishment's table. Further, that we should get our own table together and eat modestly, but well. The blogger went on to declare that the black population in the US being 44 million means that their market can accommodate black-led projects in a more financially viable way. I have several things to say about that – not uncommon – view. It is correct in terms of statistics but wrong in terms of art and identity. We are British, not American, after all. We cannot abandon our place in society nor our voice in the wider market place, in order to live self-sufficient artistic lives in the shadow of our white fellow-citizens in the UK. If we seek exclusively to chase the very real black dollar in the US but neglect the next generation of black Britons emerging into the arts, we rob these fledgling artists of their older mentors and forerunners, perhaps causing them to have to start from scratch. Reinventing the wheel is something that the older generation of black British performers have accused my generation of doing and this exodus, that looks only to the United States and not to home, can only exacerbate that need for reinvention. Ghettoizing our talent in the UK, performing for an exclusively black audience, is not empowering in my book, it is reductive. Like all artists, I seek to work in as wide and free a market as possible. But, as an Afro-Briton, I also feel it's desirable to keep my feet firmly planted in the British theatre and television scene. To encourage the next generation, yes, but more to feed myself at home with the eclectic nourishment that made me an artist in the first place.

The final thing to say on working with an exclusively black cast, is that there is a real sense of support amongst us. A feeling of being understood. Not of being 'special'. Nor 'exceptional', which is what I sometimes felt at the RSC the first time I was there. To quote Adjoa, 'The thing about being in an all black company is that you are individuated again. You become you again and that is the breathing-outness of the thing . . .' Being singled-out may temporarily feel good to the ego but it is not a true reflection of your real talent level or indeed a rounded picture of your personality. Positively or negatively, liked or loathed, in this *Caesar* cast, one was taken as one was and not *ever* as a skin colour. And in that there is, to paraphrase Brutus, much freedom and liberty.

* * *

We had the growing sense that this was going to be an amazingly exciting show. Now, we added a powerfully clear opening by our soldiers Flavius and Murellus, played by the excellent Segun Akinbola and Marcus Griffiths, respectively. They followed the immensely talented Theo Ogundipe as our Soothsayer, dancing his heart out in the city square; the community of stallholders, played by our versatile cast, demonstrating the life of a busy African market – painting the scene of this hot and vibrant city, Rome; the music, creating our next, most important, layer, played by the soon to be christened 'Vibes of March', led by Tayo Akinbode; finally, the sublime movement, expertly choreographed by Diane Mitchell. Our Western movements disappeared as our freer, more expressive bodies grew into our roles, enhanced by our East African rhythms, thanks to movement director, Struan Leslie. Finally, the text supplied by Shakespeare gave us generous *carte blanche* to explore the sounds of his every word without restrictive, clipped pronunciations getting in the way.

It was a transformation that could clearly be seen by those folks who had been present at the read-through but who had not witnessed the daily rehearsals. Their reactions on seeing one of the first, full rehearsal room run-throughs of the whole play told us all we needed to know. Potentially, this was going to be a truly great production. Now all we needed was an audience.

11

Caesar the Movie

In May 2012, the *Caesar* company launched into an intense fortnight of filming. Our producers were Illuminations Media headed by John Wyver. He had been present at our symposium the summer before and had previous experience of getting RSC shows from stage to screen. The difference between *Macbeth* with Dame Harriet Walter and Sir Antony Sher and the more recent *Hamlet* with David Tennant, was that our African *Julius Caesar* had never been seen by a paying audience. It is true that we had performed for students at Lambeth College, Clapham, about half a mile from the rehearsal rooms, the week before filming began, but that was a bare-bones version – without set, costumes or even props. Successful as that was, the rough-theatre approach was not what was required here. What we faced in this filmed version was far more challenging.

We had rehearsed to fit our performances into the nine-hundred-seat RST in Stratford-upon-Avon. Stratford's largest theatre had only recently been completely refurbished and bore little resemblance to the previous RST that I remembered twenty years previously. My recollection of playing in the old space, was of a vast barn of a theatre, where the back of the auditorium was shrouded in deep shadow and the balcony seemed to recede into infinity. The last play I had seen there was a production of *Romeo and Juliet* in 2004. I had taken some young actors there after having directed them in the same play. They all felt that the staging, décor and the very space militated against any active audience participation or, indeed, engagement. I had to agree. The proscenium-arch is wonderful for *presenting* work but not so clever at allowing the audience intimate *access* to the performers.

The refurbished theatre, by contrast, is built on the thrust-stage model. This meant that the old rear-stalls and balcony areas are brought forward – bringing the back wall of the auditorium closer in. The front row of the stalls begins just below stage height. The stalls' seats are gradually raked upward to meet the back wall of the auditorium. The Royal Circle and the Upper Circles are semi-circular and wrap around the stage, which juts out from where the old stage ended. Vomitorium exit and entry ways, on an angle to the stage, are available downstage and upstage, left and right. The back wall of the old auditorium is now the back wall of the theatre café and so the whole space has an intimate, studio feel to it.

Having rehearsed to fit this very specific space, it was a job to imagine how we would reduce our acting to accord with camera-sized performances. Theatre often feels like a more projected version of the truth we express on camera. Neither allows you to get away with anything, but theatre can give you a little more leeway for generalizing emotions when you might still be searching for the character's response to a given moment in the piece. Early days of rehearsal, which you could argue we were still in, are full of these reached-for emotions as the actor tries to plot through his character's journey. It's a stage in the rehearsal process that's chock-full of hits and misses. This is why theatre needs to be a safe environment and why so many actors feel painfully exposed when they are rusty at it.

For screen work, we are generally asked to come with our characters embedded and our lines and basic choices set. There's time for experiment and directorial adjustment but nothing like the luxury of weeks of rehearsal. Now, if we try generalizing emotions on camera, it quickly becomes clear that a performance is unspecific and derivative. So the challenge for us as performers was to take the broad strokes that five weeks of rehearsals and an ignorance of audience response had given us. Then translate that into detailed, specific work that would pass muster on extreme close-up. This should be easy enough for the calibre of actor in our cast and the vast experience that we collectively represented, you might think. But challenges, like trouble, 'come not single-spies but in battalions'. Our other nemesis was the location.

In order to adequately convince us that we were in an East African locale post-1950, we needed to find a location that didn't give away the fact that we hadn't the budget to travel to the African continent or even leave Britain. The chosen location for this act of cinematic subterfuge was Colindale. The alternative to Kenya, Tanzania or Uganda was a north-west London suburb. Not just any old part of Colindale, however, but the vast, disused and frankly filthy and abandoned Chinese supermarket, Oriental City – rank with dust and bird guano and only just vacated by the rats. Glamour locations don't get much better. The fumigators had barely tidied away their killing machines, when twenty actors, in exposing African cloths, turned up to suffer hypothermia and risk contracting legionnaires' disease. And folks wonder why the collective noun for actors is 'a grumble'.

Conditions aside, this was a blast of a shoot. The foundational work of the rehearsal process was refined and enhanced swiftly because we needed to bring performances down to camera size. Instead of physically having to turn our bodies out and away from each other, opening them up, so that the audience could see or having to keep moving for fear of messing up audience sight-lines, we were now able to just speak to our fellow actor and listen without distraction.

Other advantages were, ironically, the lack of time and money. Ingenious solutions had to be quickly found for challenges we simply had no budget for, much less time to mull over. A great example of this is Brutus' moment of breakdown, when he sees the ghost of Caesar. In rehearsals it was, naturally, a dramatic, loud, frenetic and frightening moment, culminating in the physical presence of Caesar with Brutus moving around the set in order to get away from this horrifying vision. In our filmed version, Greg came up with a brilliant alternative, partly born out of budget and time restrictions and partly out of inspiration. He decided that Caesar should die on a set of halted escalators in the eerily quiet building. In stabbing him here, we had Caesar dying against the glass sides of the escalators, smearing blood in a grotesque way across the screen or sides. In the later ghost scene, Brutus looks into his lamp and sees an image of this moment against the glass of the lamp, as if Caesar's ghost were appearing in the tiny form of a reflection. Capping this great double imagery, we also had Brutus' spectacles, a prop I'd added at the very beginning of rehearsals, onto which we also projected the image of Caesar's murder and his ghostly speech:

Enter the Ghost of Caesar.

BRUTUS
   . . . Ha! Who comes here?
   I think it is the weakness of mine eyes
   That shapes this monstrous apparition.
   It comes upon me. Art thou any thing?
   Art thou some god, some angel or some devil,
   That makest my blood cold and my hair to stare?
   Speak to me what thou art.

GHOST
   Thy evil spirit, Brutus.

BRUTUS
   Why comest thou?

GHOST
   To tell thee thou shalt see me at Philippi.

BRUTUS
   Well; then I shall see thee again?

GHOST
   Ay, at Philippi.

BRUTUS
   Why, I will see thee at Philippi then.

Exit Ghost.

BRUTUS
  Now I have taken heart thou vanishest.

(JC 4.3.273–85)

It became a subtler – more sinister – moment than we could have managed otherwise, with our very limited (i.e. non-existent) CGI budget. A creative and effective solution was found thanks to Greg's quick thinking and that mother of invention, necessity.

Yet another treat that filming Caesar afforded was the intimacy of the soliloquy. Greg and I agreed that all Brutus' monologues should be done as *to camera* addresses. The viewing audience was to be his conscience, in the same way that he, Brutus, had been using the theatre audience to work through his plans and fears about the assassination.

For monologues in Shakespeare plays, I have a very simple rule of thumb: if the character is alone and talking to herself or himself, it invariably means that Shakespeare intends him or her to talk to us. After all, she is *not* alone; we're there, too. In this way, we get not only the loneliness of the character's journey through her expressed thoughts but the feeling of inclusion in her decision-making. There is, of course, an alternative take on that. An actor might choose to play the monologue interiorly, ignoring the audience almost entirely. For me, that is pretending on top of pretending. The audience knows she is not alone because they've paid cash to sit there. Plus, they struggle to engage in the rather solipsistic exercise being played out before them.

It takes nerve to speak your thoughts in this open way but it is far more rewarding and energetically surprising than a prepared, closed-off performance. The audience will listen more attentively on one night than another. The rustle of crisp packets will grab your attention one matinee, putting you off. You might find that somebody's cough draws you to address them more intimately. I love this feeling of live theatre. It is impossible to reproduce on film, I'd argue. But, looking down the barrel of the lens and speaking to the viewer are very close approximations of that theatrical intimacy.

It must be noted that it was also so cold in this dreadful place, that we had to suck ice cubes to prevent the condensed air coming out of our mouths as we exalted over Caesar's bloody corpse. The trick was trying to balance the cold air outside with the warm air in our mouths. And, of course, it goes without saying that what's most needed when freezing in a loose-fitting toga is a cube of frozen water in one's mouth. Ah, Africa, how far away you were that day.

* * *

I've hinted that film work can feel more 'natural' than its larger than life counterpart onstage. While that's true for the most part – and we certainly took advantage of the quieter choices that could be made – film doesn't have all the advantages. Film life is certainly more isolating than theatre life and the most striking manifestation of that separation is in performance. Theatre demands that you give to the audience, to your fellow actors, to your role. It requires focused energy since there is usually a large, distracting space between performer and audience. You must convey thought, idea and emotion across a chasm. A challenging, generous and energetic act of communication. Seen this way, the performer is a kind of emotion-conveying machine. TV and film demand a certain reticence, a restraint. It isn't, contrary to the general view, more truthful than theatre. But it can be less generous. And that's not to put film work down. It is vital that we don't over-signal emotions or the audience instinctively turn off – they want to work on deciphering the picture. The camera is the conveying-machine, in this case, and the performer need only supply the right amount of projected truth for the machine to do its job. In the theatre, by contrast, to reach the furthest audience member, the actor must harness all his skills of projection – vocal, intellectual and emotional – and yet keep true to the moment. The rewards are enormous, and the act of generosity performed by actor and audience lift both out of their own isolation momentarily. It is a soothing, communal experience that film simply cannot match, because it is not live.

Theatre is, in the final analysis, a place that is unique in all creation. What other creature feels the desire to gather with other creatures, to watch other creatures deal with created crises that mirror their own lives? Do birds gather in close groups, to enjoy an evening watching another bird pretending to catch the worm of his desire? They have neither the time nor the need, for this kind of abstract interaction. Yet we, of whatever social strata, are desperate to daily observe, in the comfort of our homes, say, east London communities in sad, violent and humorous life situations (*Eastenders*); or a northern English town and its fascinatingly earthy denizens (*Coronation Street*). We then gather in theatre spaces outside our homes, to sit with hundreds of other strangers, watching a representation of human life in its extreme form.

What's even more beautifully bizarre is that we have no connection emotionally or relationally with the people whose emotions we learn to care about that evening. But we quickly agree to lay aside our cares of the day or week, to engage with some stranger's grief and pain. I think that that is amongst the most glorious and life-affirming transactions, humanly speaking. A seemingly selfless act of generosity on the audience's part, that leads to them feeling a subliminal sense of reward for their altruism and empathy. They are, in turn, given two hours' respite from whatever stresses their life holds at that moment.

Sometimes the bargain made between audience and actor doesn't work out that way. However, the need for that transaction is one of the major reasons we cannot help immersing ourselves in the story, especially when it comes to live performance. Prosaic generalizations that posit that theatre is just for entertainment, escapism, or is simply about indulgent artists showing off, miss the deeper meanings and by-products of this communal, gathering ritual.

The birth of the symbolic mind has been loosely positioned around 40,000 years ago. A time came, this compelling theory goes, when humans went from being busy merely subsisting, to wanting to record their lives and to see the lives of others represented, too. Storytelling would have already been part of human, communal experience and the recounting of stories, many anthropologists believe, was the cause of the rapid development of language. The need to tell our friends, our tribe, about imminent dangers or experiences to be avoided, doubtless led to further and further embellishments of established tales. The need to hear stories about local events, as well as instructions for survival, quickly became a campfire custom, encompassing shamanic ritual and yarns told by strangers from far-off lands. Today, we still have this ancestral urge to experience that tradition of parables and fairy tales. A tradition that offers us a comfort, an admonition, a warning. A tradition that contains all the components of our modern theatre's dramas, musicals and comedies. And our TV dramas, movies and soap operas, too, fulfil that same basic function. Shakespeare understood this human need better than many of his contemporaries, yet he eschewed teaching and instructing his audience, in favour of thrilling, moving and exciting them.

* * *

Whether in the theatre or on a film shoot, there are challenges that are hard to avoid when a group of people live very closely with material they are regularly performing. It has struck me in recent years that we, as performers, understand very little of the nature of what we do, except in the most rudimentary way. In other words, we're not encouraged to talk a lot about the nature of our work and how it affects us as human beings. I've noticed that acting companies, whether in film or theatre, have a tendency to dysfunction rapidly under certain circumstances. Some of these factors are to do with obvious clashes of personalities or the management styles of a given production. But the chief cause of company and personal dysfunction is a much subtler and unspoken one. I believe the phenomena of dysfunction comes from the actor's ignorance of the need to debrief from their roles.

'Debrief' is defined in the *Oxford English Dictionary* as an interrogation after a mission, etc. The idea was first suggested to me by a couple of psychotherapist friends of mine. In training other counsellors, they role-play various emotionally traumatic scenarios, counselling the client or being the client themselves. After they have ended the mock session, they then, very formally, declare themselves to have been 'in role', stating that they are not, in fact, subject to any of the issues involved in the made-up scenario. They finish by declaring who they really are and thus they end the session as they began it, clear of whatever emotional baggage they were role-playing. In the actor's case, debrief could be described as coming down from our heightened state in performance or rehearsals and dismantling our imagined emotional world, bringing us safely back to ourselves. I know that I and my colleagues at drama school had no idea how to do this. But I hadn't realized how widespread the neglect of this vital key to our art was, until recent years.

When I've spoken to actors about this they are initially blank, until I explain that it's the opposite of getting 'into character'. They then tend to cry, 'Of course!' Followed by an anecdote of a time when they failed to debrief from some extreme role. To expand on the theory then, let's take *Hamlet* as an example. The audience are immersed in the particular world of the story for say, three hours, leaving the theatre moved, shaken, perhaps even angry. The story, setting and characters whirl around their minds – they might talk about it for hours that night and some of them will dream of its themes. It may come back to them as a flashback during the coming weeks. But wait! They have only seen three hours' 'traffic upon the stage', no more. Think what it must be like for the actors involved. They have to dredge these emotions from within: fratricide – incest – murder – ghosts – revenge – violence – suicide – madness – and lust. This, for at least three to six weeks, full time, every day, then for three hours every night for weeks. If they didn't, to varying degrees, take it home with them, they'd be super-human.

I believe that companies can dysfunction just by dint of the themes they are tackling. The way around this is to debrief. To declare, like my counsellor friends, 'My name is John, not Hamlet. I don't have a father who was killed by his brother, my uncle, who then went on to marry my mother. I live with Mary, my wife, and our two boys. I don't suffer from the desire to kill for revenge.' Prosaic? Foolish? It is precisely this deceptively simple method that helps counsellors separate reality from the imagined scenario, after a training session. It helps them to separate their real client's problems from their own.

They encouraged me to try it and, after feeling initially foolish, I had a go at it. It brought immediate and unexpected results. It was after one of the early performances of the National Theatre's *Emperor Jones* by Eugene O'Neill, in 2007. This intense piece, for which I remained onstage for the duration of a crazy hour, had me chased by murderous locals; ghosts of murdered friends from my past; demons; slave auctioneers and, finally, a devil in animal form; the show ending in my character's suicide. But, just minutes after being carried off dead from the stage and quietly debriefing in the wings, I literally bounced back onstage for the curtain call, relieved to be me once more and not this traumatized man. Afterwards, many people commented on how relaxed and joyous I seemed onstage during the curtain call, in marked contrast to how I left it. It seems then that debrief works.

A couple of years after that experience, actor Tara Fitzgerald and I were chatting and I asked her how her show, which I had just seen, was going. She related that whilst the work onstage was excellent, the company, in her words, were dysfunctional. People were loath to engage or trust other members of the cast – and there was little, if any, socializing after the show.

I was initially surprised; I knew a lot of the actors, as well as the director involved. All of them were great company members; generous performers and collaborators. But then, I recalled that amongst the play's themes are disengagement, mistrust, isolation and shallowness of relationship. I tentatively pointed this out to Tara, suggesting that it wasn't the actors as such, but the play. She jumped out of her skin when I suggested debriefing. A psychologist friend of hers had, that very weekend, been asking Tara about her own method of de-role-ing. He had recently been working on a paper on the subject and had trawled through his acting contacts, only to discover that none of them had even heard of it. Strange, he thought, in a profession that was all about getting *in* to role, to not have a strategy of getting *out* of role. And the more I experience the art of acting, the more deeply convinced I am that this theory is, in fact, true.

* * *

Julius Caesar, the movie-shoot, came to a sudden end. We would miss the Colindale set, bird guano and all; the sense of guerrilla filmmaking that helped us all get through the gruelling schedule; and even the wonderful catering (OK, that might be going too far). What an enormous privilege it had been, though, to have the opportunity to whisper these beautiful words into the ears of people all over the world, wherever they gathered to watch our film. The schedule had been tight, but we had managed to get through the scenes as planned, despite the odds. The film could not be completed however, until we had shot the *public* scenes. The opening and closing scenes – and, of course, the most famous scene of oratory brilliance in Shakespeare's canon – the Forum Scene. For this we needed an audience and a theatre, so we packed up our costumes and headed back to Clapham. It was going to be a treat to be warm again.

12

The John Barton Session

It hadn't been more than a fortnight since we'd been in the rehearsal room, but it seemed like a lifetime ago. The usual way around for the filming of theatre, is the precise opposite of our journey. When *Elmina's Kitchen* was filmed on location for BBC4, we had already performed it at the National Theatre, in a fifty-show run. The words were embedded in us all because of its lengthy stage life. The filming was rapid and – as usual with theatre-to-television – extremely low budget. We had only five days on that occasion to film a two-hour play. We managed it, in large part, because we were so familiar with the piece. So familiar, in fact, that I recall resetting my detailed props myself on each take, as it would have taken too long to train the one stand-by props department guy in what order I cooked, bagged and labelled my take-away food. However, on *Elmina's Kitchen*, what we didn't have to contemplate was returning to a rehearsal room for a further two weeks of work.

The truth is, getting *Julius Caesar* back on its theatrical feet in a rehearsal room seemed, to some of us, a little retrograde; possibly unnecessary. We were wrong. Greg's relaxed style of directing continued setting the easy, though detailed, tone for the next fortnight. Our time on set – far from undermining our sense of expansive, theatre-sized truth – actually had the end result of releasing the text, adding a greater sense of rootedness. We had, in effect, whispered the truth of these lines and now, like a child learning to speak, had a chance to say aloud what we had learnt to say quietly. It was clear that all of us had grown in confidence.

And to cap off this fortnight of rediscovery, we had a session with the late John Barton, a legendary Shakespearean director, verse expert and teacher. He was to give us a rare master-class on the Sonnets.

* * *

Greg, wisely, hadn't put any pressure on us to quickly grow our performances for the new space. We teased nuances from lines that had been all too familiar before the filming began. Now, those well-embedded words were being new-coined. This was interesting to do and ultimately necessary, to make the lines our own again. But there comes a time when a company feels that it has had enough of playing for each other. We had all reached that moment. It felt like we needed, badly, to get in front of an audience in order for the play to breathe again.

But there's really nothing like an expert of John Barton's calibre to cause you to feel that what you thought you'd covered adequately was, in fact, only scratching the surface. As always with Shakespeare, we only get to the end of being surprised by him, when we come to the end of our intellect in dealing with his work. A comfort this, because we were being asked to live with this one play for the best part of a year. It was encouraging for us to know that there was plenty of good stuff yet to be mined.

John Barton is an RSC legend. Though I had not had the privilege of working with him the last time I was at the RSC, he was talked of in reverential terms, even back then. His roll-call of past students is truly impressive. Some cast members were invited to his flat in central London, as he was quite frail at the time. My schedule as Brutus, however, disqualified me from attending any of those sessions. Everyone who had the privilege to see him at home said that their time with him was extraordinarily enlightening. And so, it was with a mixture of curiosity and some trepidation that I took my place in the circle of chairs in the rehearsal room. Greg's suitably elegiac introduction to John did little to settle my fear that now, on the eve of opening the show in Stratford, Barton would declare that I was the worst verse-speaker he'd ever heard and insist that I be recast immediately. While that may sound a bit over-the-top, I also live with the constant fear that someone is going to tap me on the shoulder one day and gently inform me that the game's up, that I should leave the acting profession for good. I once pointed this out to Antony Sher, presuming he'd just laugh at me. But, to my surprise, he assured me that my sentiments had even been expressed by actors of the highest calibre; actors you would never dream harboured such insecurities. I'm always genuinely glad to get to the end of any job, no matter how much I've enjoyed it. It's such a relief to know that I have completed a contract without being sacked . . .

We had all had a sonnet handed to us, but I had swapped mine with Adjoa's. I can't now remember what that other one was, but its meaning seemed really obscure to me. I simply felt I could do without the pressure. So the sonnet I was left with was Sonnet 17.

Who will believe my verse in time to come,
If it were filled with your most high deserts?
Though yet heaven knows it is but as a tomb
Which hides your life, and shows not half your parts.
If I could write the beauty of your eyes,
And in fresh numbers number all your graces,
The age to come would say 'This poet lies,
Such heavenly touches ne'er touched earthly faces.'
So should my papers, yellowed with their age,

Be scorned, like old men of less truth than tongue,
And your true rights be termed a poet's rage
And stretchéd metre of an antique song.
But were some child of yours alive that time,
You should live twice – in it, and in my rhyme.

John's take on the speaking of sonnets was illuminating. I had only heard snippets of his theories over the years and they boiled down, in my ignorance of the horse's-mouth facts, to this: speak the lines all the way through to the full stop without breathing. Nonsense, of course – his theories are far subtler than that. But that's what happens in a relatively small profession: lessons are boiled down to their – often incorrect – essentials and rumour becomes the truth.

What John Barton actually says in approaching Shakespeare is this: **Shakespeare never writes sentiment, but story.** If you can find the narrative in what the characters are saying to each other or to themselves, you can be more certain of the meaning of what they say. **Shakespeare uses metaphor in order to best express a specific thought, not just poetry for its own sake.** Metaphors are constructed in the flow of the moment, not thought-through and carefully laid out beforehand. John also went on to point out: **Shakespeare often uses antithesis to open up the argument in a sonnet and puns to heighten antithesis.** We are flooded with rhymes in sonnets so we should look for and emphasize them, not shy away from them. **Sonnets nearly always start with the answer to an unheard question.** What should I compare you to, I wonder, my love? 'Shall I compare thee to a Summer's day?' Or, tell me why I should have your child, lover? 'From fairest creatures we desire increase.'

The question is sometimes within the sonnet itself. Sonnet 17 starts with a question, arising from a concern for the future: 'Who will believe my verse in time to come?' The poet goes on to answer the question in the negative, saying that time will judge them harshly as overblown rhetoric. The use of the double-entendre adds a sense of mischief to the poet's attitude: 'Though yet heaven knows it is but as a tomb / Which hides your life, and shows not half your parts.' There, Shakespeare adds a bit of nudge-nudge wink-wink humour to the serious tone of the sonnet, after a slightly ponderous opening.

I read it or rather recited it, from memory, to Adjoa who happened to be beside me. She was suitably charmed by it and we raised a laugh. I hate to be very heavy about stuff that seems to be fraught with 'moment' – it is a mechanism of protection and, I sometimes think, a kind of cowardice – but it often works in tense situations and this was no exception. The fact that John Barton thoroughly approved of my humorous reading of Sonnet 17, and gave me the opportunity to do it again, was extremely gratifying.

Out of that session, I took the following lessons: *Shakespeare asks us to be both naturalistic and heightened.* This led to another, closely related, thought that still resonates with me: *Onstage, we are asked as performers, as artists, to be both generous and genuine at all times.* The exhausting, thrilling and relentless call of theatre is just that. It is why we give so much energy to it every night and why some of us cannot do it for the duration of our careers.

Many brilliant film actors have ceased to do theatre, citing all sorts of reasons for this. Some claim that it is unreal posturing, devoid of truth; others say they'd 'like' to do some theatre, but finding the 'right projects' stymies them and certainly, in some cases, this must be true. One, Oscar-winning, film actor told me she hated the un-collaborative hierarchy of theatre; in contrast, presumably, with the egalitarian film set . . .? Regardless of their given reasons, for many, the thought of repeating with as much generosity as you can muster, the same large and profound emotions, every night for weeks, perhaps months, is a frightening prospect to consider. A dancer can physically get through a long run on adrenalin and power, a singer can use their vocal techniques to hide behind, when they are having an off night. But an actor is exposed, nightly, with nothing to protect them but their imagination. If that imagination, that creative energy, is missing one night, it makes for a very long evening indeed. A painful ordeal, in fact, for the actor trapped inside a performance he or she feels inadequate for; an actor filled with the agonizing sense that the audience that night knows they don't have what it takes. Terrifying. The fact that, for the most part, the audience is oblivious to these tortuous thoughts, does not diminish them in the least. It is said that an actor burns as many calories in a two-hour show as a labourer on a building site in eight hours of hard graft. We may, jokingly, collectively refer to ourselves as 'a grumble', but the emotional depth, physical energy and vocal power we generate each night is nothing short of monumental. And that enormous, theatrical challenge was what awaited us, as rehearsals in our home-from-home came to an end on Friday, 18 June 2012.

The costumes we used for rehearsals were packed away. The rehearsal space cleared for the next show coming in. The props that we would need for the coming months were being transported in a massive container lorry – the evocatively named pantechnicon. Finally – a little sadly – the rehearsal set was dismantled, recycled for some other show, no doubt, but never to be seen again in that configuration.

And so, to Stratford; to the place where we would be finally opening the show.

13

Stratford-upon-Avon

Entering the Royal Shakespeare Theatre, on the Sunday before our technical rehearsals began, was a thrilling moment. Of course, we had seen the small, cardboard model on the first week of rehearsals. But, that mock-up was no match for the real thing. Our ingenious designer, Michael Vale, had built the set along the lines of the back of a rundown African stadium. It was the kind that I had actually seen in South Africa, with crumbling plasterwork and rough, grey, breezeblocks. It gave a sense that little care was taken with the back of this structure, because all that was important was the show inside. It was a mirror of the world Caesar had created.

Our Africa, as exemplified by Michael's set, was a place of huge monuments and negligible pastoral care. A place where the dictator, the great conqueror, had surrounded himself with greedy sycophants, who had siphoned off the resources of a prosperous country for their own venal ends. The back of the set was surrounded by what looked like a rusty, galvanized metal, back wall – like the shanty towns of Soweto where the ordinary people of Rome lived. And surmounting the *bleachers* of the stadium, a monstrously huge statue of Caesar, arms raised in *'Veni, Vidi, Vici'* pose. The front apron of our set had several raised platforms, awkward to play at first, but we soon came to love the dynamism that their versatility afforded.

Our musicians would be placed on the upper steps of the set, giving a very present sense of the sounds of Africa that, without their considerable skills, could only be approximated. Musical Director Tayo Akinbode had assembled a fine group of players: Roger Inniss, bass; Ntshuks Bongo, saxophone; Chartwell Dutiro, mbira; Kidjali Kouyate, kora; Joseph Roberts, lead guitar and Vieux (Ansoumana) Bagayogo, djembe. Their contribution cannot be overstated. If not for them, we would have struggled to lead the audience into the atmosphere of this fictional country we had created. An unspecified African country it might be, but it needed a specific flavour to make it a real place. Nothing is more specific than the musical styles of each African nation. What Tayo achieved, therefore, with his eclectic band and its combination of skill and innovation was invaluable to our production.

Of course, some critics baulked at the idea of a fictional African country. As if setting it in Uganda or South Africa would have made it any clearer.

All that happens in that case is the audience ask awkward, unnecessary questions: 'Which one is Amin? Why are there no white people? What was the effect of colonialism on this country?' All valid questions in another context. But not specifying the country actually freed us to deal with the essence of the play. We could thoroughly investigate the elements of chaos that dictatorship incites, without being bogged down in a lot of irrelevant history. As Cyril pointed out, 'Few would complain if we set Bertolt Brecht's play *The Resistible Rise of Arturo Ui*, in an unspecified country, though it's, ostensibly, set in Chicago. After all, it's a play about how power corrupts, anywhere.'

The other vital constituent that we hadn't enjoyed before was our community chorus. They comprised around fifty black performers from the surrounding areas of Birmingham, Warwick and Coventry, put through their paces by our assistant director, Gbolohan Obeisan, who instructed them in their responses in the Forum Scene; a feat of crowd management that I did not envy. They were drilled in the impromptu African dancing that kicked our show off in just a few sessions. I have stated earlier how much Diane helped shape the world we were trying to build and nowhere was this work more clearly delineated than with our chorus of supernumeraries.

These folks hadn't received the weeks of physical and creative honing that the cast had. They had not been privy to our early stumblings over movement and accent, with Struan Leslie and Penny Dyer, respectively. So, they were thrust straight on to the stage at Stratford with little preparation. It must also be said that many of the members of the chorus had not had much stage experience at all. A monumental challenge, then, that they and the infinitely patient Gbolohan met head-on, carrying it off with aplomb. I will always be grateful for the enthusiasm, professionalism, and sense of fun and encouragement that this ensemble brought to the show and to me personally. They made me feel that even if we were the only souls who got what we were about, that would be good enough for me. And so, our complete ensemble had finally solidified.

I had installed myself in a little cottage across the road from stage door, the actor's and technician's entrance. Glad of the short walk this allowed when we got into the meat of the technical rehearsals and first previews. I love techs mainly because the pressure is off the performers and is, instead, all on the techies. We've had our time and now it's theirs, but it still means that you can try things out; testing the boundaries of the space, in terms of sight-lines and acoustics. It struck me from the very first tech I ever took part in, that it was akin to Christmas Eve – all the lights and decorations are being prepared and arranged. Anticipation and nerves are mixed with an excitement that soon this place will be filled with a crowd of people who had never seen what we had in store for them. In the tech, we get to try on our costumes, make final adjustments to quick changes, entrances and exits; performing our roles using the minimum energy required.

My favourite thing is to just sit under the lights, gazing into the darkened auditorium; filling my imagination with the world we have invented, the world in my head. The rehearsal room is always slightly distracting, in that you see the director making notes, the other actors waiting to enter, the visitors coming and going, the stage managers, heads bobbing up and down, checking that the lines and moves are as you have rehearsed them. A busy space; not very private. And so, the theatre during tech is bliss. The auditorium was like a blank canvas that I could fill with the flora and fauna of Rome or the buildings that surround this town square; imagining the shoppers going about their business; or the secret police hiding behind pillars, spying on the populace; the walls of my orchard in the dead of a Roman night, after a wild storm. I think it is the zenith of the weeks of preparation in the rehearsal room, though some actors find it a little alienating. They lose the sense of intimacy, of playing, and find it hard to focus on the story again.

A cast usually find that the dress rehearsal is when they begin to get a sense of the show being truly theirs again. Though there's always a hint of sadness, too, as it's the last time we can perform for the sake of performing; a moment that's lost from that point on. Now, people pay to see the show, so the time of messing around is, essentially, over.

A major component of any tech is experimenting with acoustics; finding our vocal levels by trial and error. Though it's important to note you can never really tell what nine-hundred people will do to the resonant quality of any space until they're sitting there. We were fortunate in having the best voice team I have ever had the privilege of working with. They were constantly in the auditorium, ready to give us tips and insights, whenever there was a lull in the tech. Generally speaking, I tend to lose the very top range of my voice after the first few weeks of a long run, especially if I have to shout or have a vocally charged speech to give, again and again. I've gotten used to this vocal 'drop-out' over the years and know that to panic about it is only to put myself in danger of losing even more range. Nervousness brings tension, tension affects the voice negatively, restricting the vocal openness and freedom you need to express powerful emotions, on a nightly basis. However, with the help of Lyn Darnley, RSC Head of Voice, and her great team, especially Nia Lynn, I managed to get through the entire run without losing any range, tone or depth, which was miraculous. The most effective method, amongst all the other tricks Lyn gave us, was one she called 'bubbling'. I had noticed, in the early days of rehearsals, that Ray and Cyril seemed to be constantly drinking out of cups, with large straws protruding out of them. I figured it was their way of taking in more liquid, until I had my first session with Lyn. She showed me a technique that had its origin in a Scandinavian speech therapist's methodology.

One of the main reasons our voices get tired is that we fail to use our breath properly. The best way to project is not to simply use your diaphragm to *push* the sound out, but to use the natural breath to *float* the sound off your throat and out of a relaxed mouth. The resonance you get from this is easily more powerful and effective than you'd get from merely pushing from your guts and a restricted throat. Plus, using the breath in this way avoids tiring and rasping the throat, thus losing range within days. The 'bubbling' technique is the best method I have come across, so far, to engage the breath in making sound.

You take a large drinking cup with a secure, preferably domed, lid and a slightly outsized straw, and fill the cup with about a third of water. Blowing into the straw with a relaxed jaw and a loosely closed mouth elicits a vibration in your cheeks. After eight repetitions of this, you then do the same, but with a little sound – a gentle hum. When that cycle's completed, you use a two-tone, high and low sound and a circuit of eight more repetitions. The penultimate stage, is to run through your whole range – high-to-low – eight more times. Finally, you hum a tune, say, 'Happy Birthday', and that ends the cycle. You will find your breath naturally flowing over your throat; the back of your throat will be relaxed; and, most importantly, the voice will be forward in the mouth, instead of sitting on your larynx. I credit this simple, fun, method with the fact that I suffered less with my voice on this show than during any I had done in over twenty-five years. Lyn and her team were always on hand, too, for help with acoustics and the fine details of verse-speaking, in the spaces we were going to be visiting on our future tour. But for the moment we only had thoughts for opening night in Stratford. Followed by the dreaded press night.

* * *

Press Night. The night when journalists descend on a theatre; when critics sit and pass judgement on the performances, set and concept we have worked so hard on. The doors are finally opened to the general public, too, and we hope that they get the fact that we have tried our hardest to make what we're doing clear, exciting and affecting. There's no telling what anyone outside of our inner circle will make of what we do. We cannot, as I've expressed earlier, write a note to the spectators telling them why we've made this choice on this line, or that decision on character or accent. We present our gift and trust that the majority of folks will come away satisfied with what we have offered to them. I've always been a bit ambivalent about this ritual. It seemed, from the very first press night I experienced on my first job out of drama school, the cruellest of all trials in art. My first professional play, *Raping the Gold* by Lucy Gannon, was in the tiny Bush Theatre in Shepherd's Bush. At that time, the Bush was above a pub on the Green; it seated roughly sixty people. You could not escape the pen-scratchings on notepads in a space that small. I remember, too, the sudden nerves that hit the small cast as the day approached. The previews had gone well, so we must have known that it was a decent production. But the fact that it would now be written about and people who had not even seen it would read about it, deciding whether it was worth buying a ticket for was, frankly, alarming. I've tried ignoring it – doesn't work. I've tried giving all my energy to that night – no, doesn't work either. The only remedy seems to be to try to hold on to what you know about the story and how you want to tell it; to hope that you hit all the right spots for the performance to at least approximate your best intentions for the piece. Then stand back and watch what happens. Not very empowering, I know, but the performer, the director, designer and the whole team have little choice in the matter.

In the case of *Julius Caesar*, we had even less idea what to expect of the audience because a Stratford audience is noted for being made up of a most international gathering of individuals. The only possible equivalent to this is Shakespeare's Globe on London's South Bank. So many tourists from all over the world descend on Stratford for the whole Shakespeare Experience and not many of them have come to see a specific play. That means that they may not know what to expect from the night's offering. Since we were not doing a traditional version, we may have had a slightly hostile – dare I say resentful – crowd on the first preview. One of several, press-free, previews before the press night. First previews have their own unique character, by the way. The audience tend to be mainly those who have heard about the play and wish to see what all the fuss is about, plus subscribers. The RSC has a host of loyal fans, subscribers, who will come to anything the RSC put on; like football supporters: positive and affirming. You really cannot set any store by the reaction of this audience, great though they are, as they tend to be predisposed to be immensely encouraging.

The second preview, the traditional 'come down' night for actors, is usually a slightly better gauge of an average audience's mood. But you still have the hangover from the night before – mostly artistic rather than alcoholic – and that colours the feel of the night, too. By the fourth or fifth preview, the confidence of everyone has grown immensely and, consequently, the daily note sessions from the director grows shorter. The points that need working become more specific until, eventually, the show is left to its own devices. Then comes the almost unexpected nervousness of press night.

I don't recall much of that night's performance of *Julius Caesar* except to note that the play seemed to go well and the audience responded positively. Actors tend to say of press night that the audience are a little tense because you have friends and family willing everything to go well. Some have already seen it, so any surprise moments are met with a neutrality that can at times seem flat to the actors. Cleverly, Greg's policy is to always put aside a performance during the previews as a separate evening devoted to friends and family. He considers that then the actors can be focused on the task in hand on press night, without worrying if their mum, partner or child is enjoying the show. It works pretty well, except it does give a bit of a downbeat feel to press night after the build up to it. Anti-climactic, is how I'd describe that evening. But still, it was finally over and we could look forward to settling in to merely performing the show every night.

I rarely read reviews as I find them, negative or positive, off-putting. But reading a couple recently, I note this from Kate Basset writing for *The Independent*:

> Feel the heat. The RSC has just set *Julius Caesar* thrillingly ablaze. Shakespeare's Roman play is often, wrongly, considered cold and colourless. Now, though, this political drama is scorchingly reinvigorated in Gregory Doran's staging which – with a superb ensemble of black British actors – translates Ancient Rome to modern-day Africa. It's a startlingly close fit ... a resounding triumph for the RSC's artistic director-designate and an outstanding contribution to the World Shakespeare Festival 2012.

There was, undoubtedly, the odd negative critique, too, but the general mood of the establishment press was positive. Of African and Afro-Caribbean takes on the show we have this from Gillian Fisher writing for *Afridiziak Theatre News*:

> This production not only presents a compelling image of East Africa in 2012; it is also a testament to Shakespeare's genius. His understanding of human nature and command of language is truly unrivalled in its ability to transcend time, culture and location. An absolute triumph of a tragedy.

* * *

It was at some point in these first few weeks that we heard intimations that representatives from Russia's Moscow Art Theatre were to visit us, in order to assess whether our production would be a good fit for the Chekov Theatre Festival they planned for the winter of 2012. Not only that, but a contingent from the United States was also due to come over to see if we might be producing a *Julius Caesar* worthy of investing a US tour in. And so, the pressure was on to continue the high standard of performances. Though, naturally, only a few of the lead actors were privy to the information that we were to expect such prestigious visitors.

On one of those Stratford nights – the same night the Russians were in – we had a visit from RSC President HRH Prince Charles. He happens to also be an acquaintance of Greg's and so comes to see shows at Stratford in a very informal way. In Act 2 Scene 1, when Brutus is trying to reason through his next course of action concerning Caesar, he declares a strong republican sentiment. I had always accompanied this line with an aggressive, dismissive gesture downstage right, along the line of the exit. That night I remembered, just before that moment came, that I had seen Prince Charles was sitting in the very aisle seat that usually received the full brunt of the aggressive gesture with the line, 'My ancestors did from the streets of

Rome / The Tarquin drive when he was call'd a king.' I wondered what he made of that line and whether he thought I had gestured in his direction on purpose. I did get to ask him afterwards whether he had enjoyed the play. Bit of a leading question, I guess, since in my experience everybody who is asked this question by an actor in the play answers in the affirmative. Or most do. As the actor Patrick O'Kane reminded me recently, 'No one comes backstage to say you were shite' . . . Prince Charles' response was that he had indeed enjoyed it and it had brought back memories from when he had studied it at school. I replied that I bet he had hated the play back then. His eyebrows rose slowly and he responded that I was right, he had detested it. 'Bad teacher . . .', he mumbled. The fact is that he is not alone. I can't recall if I had time to tell him, but if I had my way, I would ban any introduction to Shakespeare before a live play has been experienced by that novice. For example, I would be sure that any pupil first approaching Shakespeare's plays would see at least a filmed version of the play they are tackling. Best of all would be a live performance, obviously.

Failing either of those opportunities, here's a great suggestion from my friend, actor and writer Ian Flintoff: a session where an active speaking of a few choice Elizabethan phrases, littered liberally with 'thous' and 'thees', should be given to the pupils, just to give them the taste of the new language. A line here and there of Shakespeare, utilizing phrases that have entered the vernacular, could be used to build short scenes. These lines are legion and would surprise most pupils with their colloquial feel. 'Cruel to be Kind' (*Hamlet*), 'Love is Blind' (*The Merchant of Venice, The Two Gentlemen of Verona, Henry V*), 'Knock, Knock! Who's there?' (*Macbeth*), 'The world is my oyster' (*The Merry Wives of Windsor*), 'Break the ice' (*The Taming of the Shrew*), to name just a few. But getting people involved in human interactions, whether they are participants themselves, or spectators experiencing a live performance, is essential for an understanding of what Shakespeare intended. Live, the words and their meaning are given social, relational and, above all, emotional context.

In short, I believe that Shakespeare would be turning in his grave if he knew that the majority of people who first come to his plays, come to them via the classroom. Dry text, read by uninterested and uninformed students, just as ignorant of how to speak this stuff when they enter the classroom as they are when they leave it. It is as if, in a hundred years, in order to understand the phenomena of soap operas, we were asked to read a script in class of, say, the British soap *Eastenders*. In order to get a feel for this work, we'd surely have to see it first. Reading it could never give us the humour, violence and sheer speed of it. We would leave the classroom vowing never to see a show like this one and certainly never to go to the dreadful East End. Not the greatest analogy, perhaps, but you get the point. Art needs to be seen in its intended context to be truly understood – not read about third-hand in a classroom.

It does strike me as poor that our leading playwright, William Shakespeare, the one we hold up to the entire world as a beacon of British artistry, lyricism and passion, is hated and feared by the vast majority of pupils in his own country. Unless we are fortunate enough to have had an inspired and inspiring teacher, this is the case for most of us. I have met too many adults who have shied away from Shakespeare because, as children, they had received stilted, incomprehensible, instruction in his work. It is surely beholden on all British schools, at primary level onward (why not before?), to find a lively and vibrant method of passing this passion for Shakespeare on to their pupils. As Mrs Bird did for me. We should have great sympathy for British children traumatized by Shakespeare, by the way. After all, in non-English-speaking countries, Shakespeare is generally presented in a modern, translated version. So much easier than our 400-year-old text. British kids deserve to get all the help they can to find their way to the heart of these great works.

* * *

Our company's contribution to the passing on of a passion for Shakespeare was a week of filming extracts for a BBC Education Department programme on *Julius Caesar*. The format was fairly simple. We were filmed discussing the themes in a particular scene. Then we'd play the scene simply, examining the themes again, afterwards replaying the scene using exercises devised by our assistant director, Gbolohan Obeisan. It was both satisfying and frustrating, this filming week. It was exhausting to have to go through the play again in minute detail in the afternoon and then perform the same scenes again at night. I'm not sure if I'd agree to do the same thing again while performing in an equally draining show. Tiredness was already beginning to sneak up on me; I could feel that the long stretch before us was going to test every ounce of my stamina, both artistic and physical.

And, basically, I was really missing home. The summer holidays had started and my family were going away without me. It was great to know they were getting a break but frustrating not to be able to join them. That is part of the actor's lot but, obviously, not the best part. It certainly isn't conducive to a happy home life and might go some way to explaining the high level of relationship break-ups there is amongst actors.

* * *

On a brighter note, we learnt that the Russians, specifically the producers of their Shakespeare Festival, were excited by our production and were confirming an invitation to perform at the famous Moscow Art Theatre in November 2012.

This was an amazing piece of news, on top of the great reviews and almost universal approval that the show was now receiving. A rare moment in my career. I've had shows that I've loved, but not many other people in the profession have clicked with. Or shows that my fellow actors and directors enjoyed immensely that received scant praise and little success outside of the profession itself. It was not common for me to be part of a show that seemed to have critical, public and professional praise all round. A moment to savour.

And so, I ran the streets and lanes of Stratford, skirting the River Avon as it wound its way through the Warwickshire countryside. I shopped in the quaint little town. When time allowed, I relaxed in the tiny yard at the back of my rickety cottage, soaking up the sun's rays before plunging myself every night, and twice on Thursdays and Saturdays, into the darkness of the theatre. Finally, I slept peacefully in my wonky cottage as the days turned into weeks and our triumphant Stratford run finally drew to a close. The tantalizing joys of a London run loomed large. However, another huge and, ultimately, game-changing challenge lay before us.

14

London Calling

The RSC is one of those large organizations that has a great heart and sound intentions, but sometimes lacks the human, one-to-one, touch. One obvious manifestation of this was the occasion shortly before opening in London, when we the cast were all asked, rather surreptitiously, if we knew any way for the RSC to contact black people who might come and see the show in London. Their worry was that, without this help, we would get the kind of audience we had in Stratford; very white and largely middle class.

The gathering they set up to put this delicate question to us was, honestly, cack-handedly organized; I was truly embarrassed for them. The question wasn't a bad one; just a sad one. The RSC, as an organization, were taken to task, too brusquely, by Jeffery Kissoon, who demanded to know why it was *us* being asked to do *their* job? And why there weren't more black people in positions of influence in the RSC, who could have answered some of these questions in-house? Good points. Brutally conveyed. In the RSC's defence, they were collectively asking for solutions to a challenge that they were genuinely embarrassed about themselves. It was the gracious thing to do for us to try to answer the request.

Ray Fearon, our Marc Antony, was brilliant in coming up with organizations to contact and ways of publicizing the show in the black community that the RSC hadn't thought of yet – advertising on the Underground, making sure that we had black faces on our posters, being pro-active in publicizing the show in areas with a large black presence, etc. Others had social media accounts with many followers and these, they hoped, would galvanize support. I engaged my sister Glenda, a great business woman with a large database of African and Afro-Caribbean people, who would gladly spread the word far and wide. We requested that they make a certain amount of tickets available at slightly reduced prices for group bookings, in order to persuade less well-off people to spend their hard-earned cash on the show.

All in all, it was a successful strategy, and the Noël Coward Theatre in London's West End certainly benefitted from all of these promotional tactics. It is always desirable to be performing for as wide a demographic as possible, but particularly rewarding when the community you hail from acknowledges the work being done. The most satisfying aspect of our London success was that it was the excellence of the show that drew many black people to the play, not merely because it was an exclusively black cast. As Ray so simply and succinctly put it, 'If it's good, black people will come, if it's not, they won't.'

* * *

But, before London came a massive culture shock for the *Caesar* company. With Stratford over, and after a fortnight of rest, we set off for Newcastle-Upon-Tyne's Theatre Royal. This is the traditional home for the RSC before a London run. I think the idea is to acclimatize actors to a less tourist-heavy audience, before we hit the harsh glare of a demanding London house. And, most importantly, a chance to play on a traditional, proscenium-arch stage.

The two-week break had done little to alleviate my feelings of jadedness. I noticed signs of fatigue in the voices of Cyril and Ray in particular, and wondered if they'd both make it to London. In fact, both of them, along with a couple of other members of our tired company, had to take days off from the show in Newcastle, in order to rest their voices and bodies. The marathon was finally, inevitably, taking its toll.

When a company of actors has been together as long as we had – four months at this point – it can lead to a state of familiarity that can sometimes breed contempt. Add to this my previous observations about the themes of a play affecting the atmosphere of a company and you can, perhaps, imagine how delicate things were becoming. The odd argument, tensions in the cast and the usual irritations, on and offstage, manifested themselves. But I had seen far worse. And the cliques that had been formed were not disruptive to the show in any major way. A sad victim of our general tiredness was Ann Ogbomo, brilliantly playing Calphurnia. She was taken ill during the break and, sadly, had to be replaced by her equally excellent understudy, Samantha Lawson. The transition was smooth enough, but on some nights during that Newcastle fortnight, it felt like the play had taken a leave of absence and come back completely altered, so many were the cast changes. But, because this talented company was able to adjust so quickly, we generally got through it well. I won't pretend, however, that I was still feeling joyful about the six weeks in London looming before us.

It felt like *Julius Caesar* had never really settled anywhere. From the beginning, we had led this nomadic, constantly evolving, existence: a half-rehearsal; a film; another half-rehearsal; a Stratford run; an educational project for the BBC; a Newcastle re-staging. Next would come a London opening and, finally, a six-week regional tour. I wondered when we would find a settled home.

There were several challenges attached to the upcoming London run that are worth mentioning. Triumphing in London is like the Holy Grail for theatre companies. Good reviews in the right London papers are a near guarantee of a number one tour, a tour to the major regional theatres. Bad reviews, likewise, can sound the death knell of even the most promising of shows. So, opening a show in London, even if it might have already been well received in the provinces, brings with it an added tension. Greg Doran, however, is a seasoned campaigner when it comes to momentous occasions. His take on these landmarks, often fraught with anxiety, is to remind us that it is going to feel weird and that you might make strange errors that you've never made before. The trick is to note that you've messed up that moment and then move on. Not letting an incident in the first scene effect the rest of the evening is a great note. We beat ourselves up over things that, frankly, only loom large in our own minds. An error, even a major one, need not mean the rest of the show is a washout.

One challenge was that we had performed in Stratford on a stage that accommodated three-sided playing. The audience were practically surrounding us and that led to a three-dimensional performance, which, in turn, gave us fluidity in our stage movement and a closer approximation of 'real life' interactions. The proscenium-arch, on the other hand, is much more rigid, in that the audience needs to see the action played out to them, to mitigate against any feelings they might have of being outside of the action taking place onstage. The problem with this, especially in scenes of true intimacy, is that actors are tempted to turn outward too much, loosening the link between one actor and another.

One of the major casualties of this was my relationship with Cassius/ Cyril. I felt a greater distance from him than I had ever felt during either rehearsals or the Stratford run. It seemed to me that I had stepped out of the play and was watching some performances becoming larger and larger as the pull of the proscenium setting caused a less subtle style to creep into everything taking place onstage. I'd be surprised if I wasn't as guilty of this as everyone else. It is very difficult, once the moorings have slipped on a show, to get it back to where it was before. I was left feeling more and more disappointed that we couldn't have reproduced the spatially specific Stratford setting, here in London. And on top of the already tricky circumstances, it emerged that the Noël Coward Theatre – and indeed all subsequent theatres in our future tour – could not accommodate the original set with its stepped staging. The front apron of the stage, forward of the end of the bleachers, was flat and foreshortened. This meant that the playing areas were greatly restricted and gave the scenes a two-dimensional, rather than a three-dimensional feel, physically and sometimes – especially early on in the London run – emotionally, too.

An additional issue we faced was the loss of our community chorus. I'm not altogether sure why some provision could not have been made to continue their presence with us. However, amongst some of the reasons given were a lack of dressing-room space and the costs of hiring folks commuting to and from Birmingham, Coventry and Warwick for every performance. We could, feasibly, have engaged a London-based community chorus but that would certainly have meant more rehearsal time. Looking back, I now find it strange that we, as a cast, didn't put up much of a fight over this, but it has to be said that Ray and I truly felt their loss in the Forum scenes.

However, the most telling loss was the change in the show's structure. Greg had decided very early on to forgo an interval and drive the play straight through from the assassination of Caesar to the very end line. He hoped that, in this way, the anti-climactic feel to the second half of the play, which many folks had complained about over the years, could be ameliorated. Once Caesar is dead, we have, post-Forum Scene, the Triumvirate ironing out the future of Rome, followed by the in-fighting that destroys the Cassius/ Brutus relationship. In our Stratford version of the show, the play drove through from the Forum Scene and Antony's rousing 'Friends, Romans, countrymen' speech, into the resultant mob violence, culminating in the death of the innocent poet Cinna.

In London, unfortunately, we lost a great deal of the story's drive by having an interval just after the end of Caesar's assassination scene. Having said that, I think that if you must have an interval in this play this is probably the place to put it. We all know that Caesar is going to die. What we don't remember is what happens after. But, in our case, we could harness the memory of what we had learnt in Stratford's interval-less version, and that energy might capture the audience for the second half. By and large, we did that – highlighting how different the world of the great dictator was from the world of bickering leaders, post-assassination. It helped to clarify one of the major thrusts of our take on *Julius Caesar*. The post-dictator vacuum is always trickier to negotiate than the revolutionaries have planned. And Shakespeare, in *Julius Caesar*, is amazingly prophetic, mirroring so clearly what happens in many revolutions. The leader is assassinated or exiled and bitter rivalries, factions and civil wars rush in to fill the vacuum the absence of the Strong Man has left. Events in North Africa and the Middle East, around the time that we were both rehearsing and performing, were strangely reflective of Shakespeare's play. As we saw Libya, Syria, Tunisia and Egypt go through the death throes of long-term dictatorships and try, increasingly desperately, to form some kind of coherent government, we sensed that zeitgeist had met creativity, in the shape of our *Julius Caesar*. It really was, to echo what the actor John Kani had long ago pointed out to Greg, *Shakespeare's African Play* but also, given current events, it could be argued, *Shakespeare's Universal Play*.

The great shame was that the loss of our interval resulted in a gradual stretching out of our playing time. From a show that was running at two hours and twenty in Stratford, we were, with a twenty-minute interval, closing in on two hours and forty-five minutes. This might not seem like that long an overrun, but – believe me – it lessens the emotional punch of a show when it stretches our concentration for longer than is necessary. The question is: why did we have to change the format in the first place? The answer is so prosaic it almost beggars belief. In Stratford, the lack of an interval was not a problem because no financial loss was suffered at the bar, since it remained open for a post-show concert by Tayo and 'The Vibes of March' – a gig that was always well attended. London, by contrast, did not have a bar open post-show. Therefore, they greatly relied on the audience buying drinks in the interval. I heard a credible rumour that to have sustained the six-week run without an interval in London would have meant the RSC compensating the Noël Coward Theatre for loss of bar earnings, to the tune of £40,000. A sum that they, naturally, didn't want to cough up. The real shame is that artistic concerns had to take a back seat to financial ones. We have to hope that a day will dawn when the opposite might be true.

* * *

I passed a very strange fortnight just before we closed the show in London. It had gone well and we were sold out for the run. No mean feat, in a time when, due to the London 2012 Olympic Games, the West End was struggling to keep shows open, even with major names on the bill boards. Unfortunately, our performances were showing major signs of fatigue. The running times grew longer still and strong feelings of alienation began to assail me. I couldn't believe some of the scenes in the way I had in rehearsals and I felt that over-acting was beginning to creep in to all our performances. This can happen on long runs. Factions and bickering, though mild, started to rear their ugly heads, again. Friends who came to see the show were noticing that the Cassius/Brutus relationship was difficult to fathom, as Cassius seemed too over-emotional and Brutus too stoical. How could there be a deep friendship, let alone a life and death love-bond, between two such polar opposite men? A fair question and one I could not answer. The only thing I could do was try to remain true to my original vision of Brutus, act as honestly as possible, and hope that the grounded performance coming from me would affect the larger performances around me. I think, however, that what really happened is that I withdrew into a reality that isolated Brutus and me in a protective, but unhealthy, way.

Isolation is the worst place to create from, especially in a collaborative art such as acting. It wasn't the first time that I'd experienced these feelings – drama school held a few of these moments of artistic crises for me. I cannot trust a scene that I'm in if I jump out of it and observe an actor *acting*. It just puts me outside of the story and leaves me unable to engage with any degree of conviction. The ensuing panic has me protecting myself, by being hyper-concentrated on believing my own story. The exclusion of others is inevitable. In this case, it could only be detrimental to the story as a whole, if the lead character, and the actor playing him, felt himself to be in a separate play. One where the realities he was faced with in his world were those of an honest man in a world of falsehoods. It kind of works as a way to play Brutus, but was nowhere near as much fun, or inclusive, to perform. Talking to Cyril later, I know that we were both suffering from this feeling of isolation, though we chose very different methods of coping with it. Missing our director was at the root of the problem, but this was not clear to either of us at this point.

It wasn't all flat-lined gloom however. There were also very funny, albeit dark-humoured, incidences that kept me going for a while, in this increasingly difficult period. I had invited my old friend, Nigel, to come and see the play. I had forgotten when he was coming, though, and so I was pleased to receive his note to say that he'd be in that night. I had also received a text from my friend Tom Hiddleston to say that he, too, would be watching that night. Tom and I had performed in the BBC TV version of *Henry V*. He was an excellent Henry and my admiration for him as an actor was high. So the mild pressure of *having friends in* was in the air that evening. I tend to like that during a long run, though, as it gives me an extra incentive to be on my mettle.

As the show began, I noticed, to my surprise, that the lights that usually dimmed on the audience as we enter as 'Caesar's Train' were up. The first sight that struck me was Tom, though seated, towering above the audience members around him, halfway up the stalls. He seemed to be lit by a strange, ethereal light that made it impossible not to spot him straight away. Looking to my right I could see that Nigel, too, was in a very prominent position in the Royal Box, at the side of the stage, all by himself. It was a little disconcerting but fine, I supposed. Until I noticed the source of Tom's unearthly 'aura': Caption Boards.

The caption boards in most theatres are to the sides of the playing area. In Stratford, they were literally over your shoulder and over the shoulder of the actor you were addressing. It's disconcerting to be speaking lines that appear in dazzling LCD over the heads of your co-actor just before you speak them. And if, as often happens, you have changed a word in the text and you see the correct word up there, you are thrown in so many ways. Add to this that the LCD is often the brightest thing in a darkened theatre, and you can perhaps imagine how annoying it is for the actors. Perhaps the most problematic element is that hearing members of the audience are drawn to read the captioned text for clarity, or simply because the words are there. The sight of hundreds of people staring above your head or to the side of the stage, when you're busting a gut to express an emotion, is tortuous. And then there's the punch lines to verbal gags, given away just before you hit the audience with them; visual gags falling flat, because half the audience were reading the text when you tripped over that bit of furniture.

And so, the fact that I hadn't been told that it was a captioned performance, before it was too late to warn my friends to try another night, was annoying. I struggled that evening to keep hold of any reality at all. I found, to my shame, that there were too many distractions to ignore in the end and I had, from my perspective, a disappointing night.

Post-show, I came out of the stage door to discover Tom and a friend of his, waiting. Our conversation was a little strained. I was so gutted that he had seen such a disjointed, awkward and unconnected performance from me. Tom, all graciousness and insight, understood what had happened and gave me the sincere encouragement that he could at least see what I was trying to hold on to, despite the obvious obstacles. I am very grateful to him for picking me up that night and I was going to need every ounce of the pep he had given me for the rest of this bizarre evening. Leaving Tom, I made my way through the late-night streets of Soho to the Groucho Club, to meet Nigel.

Groucho's is known as a haunt for people in the media. Performing in the West End meant that we as a company received a free, though temporary, membership. I'm not a massive fan of exclusive clubs or celebrity hang outs and, though I have nothing against Groucho's as such, I had met people in there before, who whilst chatting to me were, in truth, far more interested in the far more interesting people milling about behind me. However, Groucho's is quite close to the theatre and so I had asked Ben Tyreman, our fantastic company manager, to arrange for me to bring Nigel there after the show.

When I got to Groucho's, I found Nigel Goodwin, looking like he always has to me – a cross between Jesus and Doctor Who. He had encouraged me in times of crisis on a number of occasions, so I was very much looking forward to a bite of supper and a good, uplifting natter with him.

Our first obstacle was that the receptionist could not find any record of my membership, temporary or otherwise. I asked her to call her colleague who had arranged our membership, but she said that the contact name I had been given didn't correspond to any name she knew there. I called Ben, but he could only repeat the name he'd been given. The receptionist's manner was so off-hand anyway I decided not to insist and took Nigel away. And so, we started the twenty-minute walk to Holborn where Nigel could catch a train and I could walk home to my digs just around the corner.

On that walk, we talked of many things: our families, health, God, Art – all the usual subjects that Nigel and I tended to discuss when we had occasion to meet. When we finally got to High Holborn and were just about to cross the road to the station, Nigel turned to me in all sincerity, saying, in his rich, actorly tones, 'Do you know, dear Pat, I really admired your choice of accent. Welsh is so redolent of toughness and stoicism.' I was open-mouthed. I was just not used to Nigel joking in this way. But, with the following, I knew he was deadly serious: 'Yes, I knew Dylan Thomas' widow for a time; that Valleys accent is very rich, isn't it? I mean, you only have to think of Burton – and Hopkins, too; they had that kind of miner's toughness where the emotions were always in check; like Brutus, very stoical ... excellent.'

I blinked and walked behind him slightly as we crossed the road, hoping to catch a glimpse of a cheeky smile in the corner of his eye but there was none there. A couple of minutes and a change of subjects later, he was ready to leave me. That was when he chose to reiterate his admiration for my 'Valleys Brutus' and he was gone, leaving me dazed and bemused. Of course, like all actors, I'm easily undermined, so I spent the next hour or so in my digs going through each line. 'Caaasius, be not deceeeived', thinking, 'Of course, it sounds *really* Welsh!' And this self-inflicted torture went on for some time. 'Nigel actually thought that I had decided to play this African man as a Welsh émigré?' I pondered. 'In what world would that have been a sound acting choice?' The next day when, still in a daze, I related the incident to Adjoa and Cyril, their genuine laughter and total befuddlement heartened me greatly. Nigel had gotten the wrong end of the accent stick. My Brutus was far from the long-lost cousin of Tom Jones, they reassured me, after wiping tears of laughter from their eyes . . .

I think that incident, amusing though it now seems, more than any other, highlights my fragile state at that point. I could have believed anything negative. It happens on a long run, I guess, and this one hadn't nearly ended yet. The challenge of a tour to six UK towns awaited us. And this tour was to prove the catalyst for the biggest crisis of the whole *Caesar* adventure.

15

The *Caesar* Roadshow

We left the noisy, exciting, buzz of London behind and set off for our six-week provincial UK tour in the autumn of 2012. I've never really been a fan of touring – living out of a suitcase; having to plan ahead to book your mystery digs; never knowing where anything is in a new theatre, until the last day when you realize you're about to leave for another, new theatre. Most shows don't feel the same in every venue and this show had changed its stripes more than once already.

Having said that, I was pleasantly surprised at how much I liked our first touring venue. The Waterside Theatre in Aylesbury wasn't a bad way to start this new leg of our journey. Friends who hadn't managed to see the show in London came to see us here, as it is a short train journey from the capital. Aylesbury had followed a week off that had allowed me to refresh myself a little. Traces of the exhaustion that had hit me at the Noël Coward Theatre hadn't left me entirely, but I was glad that the pressure of London was behind us.

Around this time, we had the confirmation of what we had heard whispered in London and had all secretly been hoping for: we were going to America with *Julius Caesar* on a twelve-week tour, starting at the famous Brooklyn Academy of Music in New York. I say it was something we were hoping for – in fact, I was slightly apprehensive at the prospect. As I have said, I was missing home already by this point and had been away, bar about three weeks, for seven months. The thought of spending a further three months away in America in 2013 filled me with a mixture of pain and joy. It led to great tension at home and I can well understand why my wife wasn't happy at the prospect of being a single parent, to all intents and purposes, for another twelve weeks. On top of this domestic strain, I had to continue performing in this increasingly dissipated show, which was getting less and less easy to contemplate.

On the road, the show continued to stretch and become overblown, as far as I could see. I rooted myself more and more in the *reality* I had come to rely on so desperately. My relations with Cyril hadn't improved, and I had asked Ben Tyreman whether he could separate our dressing rooms from that point on. In most venues, it was possible and that helped alleviate some of the tensions of brotherly irritation. I can well believe that I was annoying the hell out of him, too, as he struggled to get me to react onstage, while I became increasingly stoical.

My lowest ebb in many ways came in Bradford. The Alhambra Theatre is a huge and ornate building. The auditorium is acoustically good but the setting not conducive to drama, in my opinion. At the end of our foreshortened stage was the gaping chasm of a deep orchestra pit. It meant us reaching out, across a divide of ten feet, to reach even the first row of the stalls – far from the intimate setting of Stratford. I struggled here the most because it felt like *Julius Caesar* had lost all meaning, except as a vehicle for indulgent performances and even longer running times. The dressing room (shared once again as room could not be found for separate ones) is usually a safe haven for the performer. But this one was as silent as the grave. Cyril and I avoiding each other, speaking only when necessary. At the time, it was hard to know the roots of this alienated behaviour on both our parts but I guessed it was possibly the consequence of having very different ways of dealing with stress and tiredness. This tension may well have been mirrored in different situations and relationships all over the show but I can only speak with any authority about what I was experiencing with Cyril. I had decided that the best strategy was to ignore the acting choices I didn't like in my fellow performers, on the grounds that there wasn't going to be anything that I could effectively do to change those choices. And dwelling on them only served to strip me of the little energy I had for the show. My issue? I think that Shakespeare is a playwright of wit and speed; the quickest person in the auditorium should feel that it is going at a pace that makes them work. If we slow verse-speaking down, so that every word lands . . . like . . . a . . . bomb, it conversely denudes the speeches and scenes of power since we diffuse the intensity with empty air. Again, this was just my opinion of some performances. No doubt I, too, was guilty of indulging in favourite moments.

That said, my anchors in all this were the wonderful Adjoa Andoh and the equally superb and inventive Simon Manyonda. Adjoa's acting was always fiercely honest and powerful. She broke my heart onstage on many, many nights; I was very grateful to her for being so consistent. Simon was a dream to work with, too; we invented more and more moments together as Lucius and Brutus. This relationship, unique I believe in the performance history of *Julius Caesar*, gave such depth to my character that I am sure Brutus would not have been as rounded a human being without it. From his first comedic scene introducing the disgruntled, teenage employee, to his sometimes hilarious, sometimes poignant, stress-induced narcoleptic episodes, Simon kept a truthful and inventive relationship going with both audience and me. I never felt upstaged at any point with him, yet I know from a lot of my friends who came to see it, and the reviews that we received, that Lucius' storyline is one that struck the audience very deeply. His affecting, emotional line was full of integrity and he rarely overstepped the bounds of taste and subtlety. In fact, whenever he did step on a moment that needed quietness and focus, I only had to tell him that I wasn't sure it worked for him to look at it again and invent something even better and subtler. He, equally, felt confident enough to tell me when I had crushed a moment of his or when I wasn't giving him time to complete a necessary piece of stage business. It was a fantastic and enormously collaborative working relationship.

The musicians were always very encouraging to us, too, and in some theatres we had them not in a darkened room in the basement, but on the same level backstage as our entrances and exits. Not to put too fine a point on it, they were an absolute godsend to me – a place where I could go to chat and laugh and be relaxed, without fear of offending or stepping on increasingly sensitive toes. Socially, it was difficult to find people I wanted to spend lots of time with. This might have been to do with the fact that I was so knackered that all I really wanted to do was crash out at my digs and sleep, or talk to my family, then crash out and sleep. The average age of the best part of the troupe was about twenty-seven and I felt that the inevitable late nights and partying were just not going to be helpful for me. The older members were pretty private, too, so it was a job to think where I most fitted in; and I really didn't need another *job* at this point. That isn't to say that I struggled to get on with anyone in particular because apart from the odd incident of tetchiness on my or another cast member's part, I got on reasonably well with everyone. I don't think anyone – with the possible exception of Cyril – could have suspected that I was under any *Caesar*-fatigue at all.

But Bradford was testing me in ways that I felt unable to fully resolve by giving myself the usual 'get on with it' pep talk. In fact, as you can gather, I was at the end of my strength. I had just about had enough of pretending I was happy to be in isolated truth, while all around me lied, and I was thoroughly sick of missing my family. If the show had been a pleasure from beginning to end, it still would have been difficult to bear the long absence from home, but given how dysfunctional it all seemed, I couldn't see any point in continuing. And with the prospect of a further three months looming – albeit at the end of a four-month break at the end of this tour – I really couldn't see any way out. Dramatic, it may have been, but it was how I felt at the time; trapped and out of solutions. I resolved to talk to Greg as soon as I could and lay my cards on the table, once and for all.

I had tried, in the days leading up to talking to Greg, to contact him via text messages and email, in order to let him know where I was at with *Julius Caesar*. It seemed to me that he had somewhat deserted us in Newcastle and that would have been the ideal place for us to get right what had become wayward. London was better, but we still lacked his presence on a weekly basis. And then, after Aylesbury, where he didn't visit at all, and the start of Bradford, I felt thoroughly abandoned. Where was the hands-on guide that we had been shepherded by since London rehearsals in March?

Greg was now the artistic director of the RSC and in rehearsals for his next show. He was making regular trips abroad, too, to try to secure both the American venues and a possible tour to South Africa. The dream of playing *Julius Caesar* in front of Nelson Mandela – since the show had been partly inspired by the great man – was a golden carrot all of us wanted to pursue. And so, it was understandable that he was taken up with these important artistic and business matters. But, the actual effect was that, instead of guiding our baby steps from thrust-stage setting to proscenium-arch, he left us to our own devices for much of the post-London run.

I have no doubt that he would have intervened earlier if he felt that the show was in such trouble, but he had no way of knowing how it was going except for the show reports he received nightly. These are the blow-by-blow accounts of each night's major events. The accident that led to injury, the lines that were fluffed, the props that broke, etc. In these reports, the director will get a vague idea of how the show is going. But they cannot hope to cover the issue of corporate morale or, indeed, individual cast members' problems. A show report cannot even attempt to convey the underlying tensions in performance or the general tiredness that can come over a cast a long way into a run of this length. The best that could be hoped for from such a document is an approximation of how the show is going. And, on the surface of things, it *was* going. We were having reasonable houses, the reviews were good; the letters and 'thank yous' were still coming in. From the look of it, what could possibly be the matter?

Therefore, it came as no real surprise to find that my first message to Greg from Bradford, asking him to talk urgently to me, was met with silence for twenty-four hours. And anything, given my current levels of sensitivity, would have been better than that. It helped to solidify my resolve to act quickly. After talking it through with my agent, I came to the decision in the middle of that Bradford week to finally consider quitting *Julius Caesar*.

I felt an immediate sense of relief and phoned home to say that I had wrestled with myself but that I had come to a calm decision to quit the show after the UK leg. If I did, I would be home for the three months of 2013 that would have encompassed the US tour and this news made my wife extremely happy – another positive, weighing on the side of getting off the *Julius Caesar* bus.

I received what I took to be a perfunctory text from Greg the next day. He said, in effect, that he was too busy to talk straight away, but would come to Norwich in three weeks' time, to take a look at what I had been saying about the show's deterioration. His text was not comforting; it seemed to me to be about keeping me calm, rather than listening to my artistic grievances. I think that he must have felt that it was just fatigue talking and would quickly pass but, unfortunately, he had underestimated my strong feelings. When I finally talked to Greg about the situation onstage and off, he seemed to accept that it had become intolerable. I intimated that I was on my way to deciding to give it a rest. He urged me to wait and see if things changed after he'd had the chance to give some long-distance notes to the rest of the cast. I assured him that it wasn't going to be a few notes that would change what had become, to my mind, an irreparably damaged show. But I promised to sleep on it for twenty-four hours.

The following show, as far as I can remember it, was another trial and I made the third, or fourth, resolution to leave the show, phoning Greg in the night to chat about it again. I ended our call by giving my promise to wait till the morning to finally decide. That morning, I sent a message to Greg to announce my departure, but only managed to leave a voicemail. Not ideal, but I didn't want to hold up the process any longer than was necessary. The edited email below is what I received in reply.

I am glad we managed to talk last night. I'm sorry we couldn't do so the previous day, as with rehearsal, and the British Museum screening, things were hectic. But I am sorry to hear that you have already come to a decision. Is it a fait accompli? It is a bit of a bolt out of the blue.

As we discussed in Newcastle, I would try my damnedest to get Julius Caesar to New York if you (and Cyril and Ray) were committed to it and would also try my very hardest to get it to South Africa. I think I made it clear that I would not go ahead without any one of the three of you. But, in particular, I could not contemplate the show without you. You are the major reason this show is a success, without doubt.

It has taken a great deal of effort, on a lot of people's behalf, to try and make a further life work, and to raise sufficient funds in a difficult year to pull this off; and a lot of diplomatic efforts, and creative thinking to contemplate a potential visit to Africa. So it is disappointing if those efforts have to be frustrated. Is there really no possibility of you reconsidering the proposition?

I do of course appreciate, as I said last night, that being away from home and family must be very hard, and I can understand if you feel the light has somehow gone out of the art, but with a four-month gap between Moscow and New York, is there not a real possibility that we could refresh any tiredness you feel?

The reason the Board have been so determined to make this work, despite the considerable odds, is that they feel very proud of the production, as we all do, and feel that the focus on the RSC, already high because of the opening of Matilda on Broadway, will be greatly enhanced by being able to present what the company should do best – Shakespeare, alongside it.

I feel your performance as Brutus deserves that international exposure, and don't want you to deny yourself that spotlight. And of course, I have to admit that, not having had my own productions seen in New York, particularly in the recent residency, I was looking forward to having a production of which I feel so proud, have such a high profile exposure. They come along so rarely, the ones you feel you got close to getting right, and which are recognized as such. From the Board's point of view, having Julius Caesar at the Brooklyn Academy of Music would be an ideal way to refresh the RSC's reputation, and herald the new regime.

I said I would reschedule any plans and come up so we could discuss this face to face, and if there is any chance of changing your mind by doing so, I will. If not, and you have indeed made up your mind, and there is no negotiating position, then I will have to institute a series of measures to extricate us from the tour, and stand down Jeremy Adams (our producer) and the team, and I would need to get on with that.

If so then I will come up a little later, and we can chew the fat, as discussed. If not, (and I do realize this decision is not just the product of a wet lonely Tuesday night in Bradford) then let's work out how we can re-engage. I'd appreciate the opportunity to persuade you.

I'm rambling. It's late.

Fondly

Greg

I couldn't help but be heartened and charmed by Greg's letter. What actor doesn't like to feel that his performance is so valued that an entire tour to the US and beyond is riding on it? Vain? You bet. But, I suddenly felt the responsibility of possibly closing the whole thing down on the strength of my fatigue and irritation with a few self-perceived, indulgent performances. A lot of people were going to be very disappointed. I had to think again. And if Greg was willing to come up immediately, then I would consider *that* the answer to my call for real help.

And so, on the Thursday matinee, true to his word, Greg came up to see the show in Bradford. I had wanted it to be a secret presence in the auditorium, but the cat was let out of the bag and the whole cast was suddenly on its collective mettle. I remember reading Fritjof Capra's book, *The Tao of Physics*, many years ago. In it, Capra describes an atomic-level phenomenon in such a way that it has stayed with me ever since. He said that, in order to study an atom's behaviour in the laboratory, the physicist must examine that atom in a contained environment. The very act of containing and examining the atom in this rarefied environment changes the very behaviour that the physicist wants to observe. I think the same is true in many situations and this was no exception. We were being observed again, at last. The show was better, the acting calmer and more disciplined and the pace was up on the usual sluggishness.

I must confess to feeling a slight resentment, that things could be improved with as little incentive as having the director in the house, but I would be lying if I said that I didn't also feel relief that perhaps I could, after all, make it to the US, if this show could be fixed. After the interval, however, the curtain refused to go up. A technical glitch in the electrical system meant that the separation between auditorium and stage, called The Iron, was stuck. For about half an hour, it looked like we were not going to be able to present the second half of the show. Someone was in the act of announcing to the audience that we would wait another ten minutes or so and then abandon the second half altogether, when a keen observer in the auditorium spotted Greg in the Circle. He was immediately asked to speak to the audience and very dutifully he came down and did just that.

At the end of his apology, charming as always, he acceded to the audience's request that the actors come out and at least take a bow for their first-half performance. So, fifty minutes after the second half should have started, we all trooped out and bowed to the house. As we came up from our second bow, the iron curtain was finally released. The audience whooped with delight at the prospect of seeing the second half. Confession time: I wasn't pleased. I thought we'd been given a half-afternoon off. I'm sure I wasn't the only one who thought that it was rotten luck, that we had to wait so long, only to be forced to go back and finish off the show, shortening our already short break between shows by an hour.

Miraculously, the second half, which had stretched from the one hour and two minutes in Stratford, to sometimes one hour and fifteen on the road, came in at fifty-eight minutes. A record never before, or since, bettered. So the gist of Greg's notes post-show was predictable:

Hi Paterson, I am sitting in a chilly waiting room at York Station waiting for a train that has been delayed by an hour! Delays seem to be the order of the day.

Thanks for coping so well with the tardy safety curtain (iron-y indeed!)

I had a good chat with Cyril. What I saw was a relationship that had been nuanced and symbiotic, become strained and troubled. I think this has been an evolution of different reactions. From my perspective it almost seems that Cassius has become needier and volatile, as he perceived Brutus become more impatient and dismissive of him. But, equally, I suspect that Brutus has become less tolerant as Cassius has become more fretful, or even panicky, and has had to dismiss him or cut him short in order to control that volatility.

Would that be a fair assessment? I don't imagine that any calibration that Cyril and I discussed in our rather rushed and truncated chat would have been evident in the show tonight, but I hope we can get back to the love that underlies that friendship so powerfully, as negotiated as it is, because it is one of the things that is most revelatory about what you have both achieved. I want you to both be able to get back to looking in each other's eyes . . . It must be very hard to feel out of step in a play in which you rely on each other so much. If there is anything more I can do to broker that any further, I will of course do so.

Let's keep monitoring how it goes. The break in a week will be a very useful breather, I am guessing.

Let me know

Love G

So, that was that. Pretty detailed notes, not all included here, that I felt helped answer some, though clearly not all, my fears about the show and the feasibility of continuing beyond the UK tour. In fact, the hardest thing about Greg's notes were the truths contained within them for me. He was gently encouraging me to take a share of the blame for the state of the show. I accepted this because he was the director. His were the only eyes that had seen the show from inception to realization. He was the only person who had sat through the deliberations about each character onstage. If there were discrepancies between what I had originally intended and what we now had, then it was fitting that Greg be the one to point those out. And so my resolve to leave after the UK tour slowly began to dissolve, as the empathic part of my personality kicked in and I began to see how things might have been difficult for Cyril, too. That didn't mean that the show was miraculously brilliant that night or even for the rest of that run in Bradford and our subsequent week in Manchester's Lowry Centre. The show still seemed out of sorts with itself. But my attitude had altered towards it. And, by Manchester, week three of the tour – week seventeen all told – I could see things possibly working out. Little did I know that a shocking blip was about to appear on the radar that could have ended all hopes of a further life for the entire show.

* * *

Arriving at our final venue of the UK tour, the New Theatre, Cardiff, was like seeing the light at the end of a very long tunnel. The penultimate venue, Norwich Theatre Royal, had proved to be something of a pleasant surprise. The audiences in Norwich were quick-witted, warm and enthusiastic. Coming back after our week-long break to be ambushed by the joy of recapturing some of my love and energy for the show, in a setting that seemed to both welcome and understand our brand of storytelling, was gratifying and a great relief.

Then came Cardiff and, again, I was pleasantly thrown by the enthusiasm and liveliness of the audiences. However, if the audience was pleasing and the show itself had found more of its life than ever, one thing still remained on the brink of disaster. My relationship with Cyril. I had come to the conclusion that my best bet was to keep my head down and play as openly as possible onstage. I had gathered that his notes from Greg had encouraged Cyril to do the same and so my confidence that we could make this work rose gradually. But that was all to change rather rapidly on our first matinee in Cardiff. Towards the end of the play, as we had rehearsed it and as the moment had grown over several months, Brutus gathers the staff of his dead friend, Cassius, and, holding it aloft as a symbol of his friend, charges off to take his revenge. The staff in this case was a thin branch of a tree that Cyril had very carefully found and worked on meticulously, as he wanted it to be his character's major prop, his talisman, in the final battle. During this sequence, I always got very emotional, naturally, and this one afternoon, smacked the staff against the floor. To my amazement, about a third of the staff broke off and went spinning in the air behind me, landing beside Cyril's prone body, missing him by inches. I breathed a sigh of relief as it was a sharp-ended shard and could have hurt him if it had landed on any exposed part of his body. However, I thought it was a funny incident that we would all laugh at later and exited as usual. As Brutus, I had used the staff at the very end of the play, raising it to the heavens to salute my dead friend and then I gently lowered it to the ground in front of me; laying Cassius to rest finally. It is the beginning of an overwhelming sense of completion and peace, reinforcing Brutus' decision to take his own life. The final scene went well, as it always had done, and we took our bows as usual.

Seconds after coming offstage, I headed to Cyril's dressing room to apologize for breaking his prop and to, hopefully, share some conciliatory humour over it. To my dismay, rather than accepting my apology, I was harangued by Cyril who seemed to be accusing me of breaking his staff on purpose. I couldn't imagine even thinking such a thing of a fellow actor, let alone telling them that I thought this might be the case. But, I hadn't fully grasped how important a prop this was for him. He later explained that he had needed a prop that spoke to him of Cassius' practical nature. A potent souvenir from his manhood initiation ceremony, where he had to bludgeon an animal to death; a rite of passage ceremony of the kind that Cyril knew took place in West Africa. And so, this found object was significant, in that it represented Cassius' connectedness to his cultural traditions and separated him, somewhat, from the career politicians of Rome. At the time, though, all I could gather was that Cyril's grievance was that he had found that staff, that he had worked it and varnished it, etc. – that my act of destruction was a typical, selfish act, indicative of all the other selfish things I had been doing throughout the run. I was flabbergasted and reiterated that I certainly didn't break his staff on purpose, adding that I did not accept his accusation of selfishness onstage. I ended the conversation as graciously as I could, with another apology for the accident and he seemed, after a while, to accept that. We left it there, but I was, to say the least, very frustrated about what I perceived to be his overreaction. However, the show must go on and that night things got very interesting indeed.

Getting to the moment of grabbing Cassius' staff at the end of the play, I struggled to find it. I then noticed a bit of it sticking out from under Cyril's prone body and went to pull it out. Bizarrely, Cyril was pressing his body down on it and was clearly trying to stop me having it, as I perceived it. I laughed openly. It seemed like a typical actor's gag and so I left it there and carried on. When I got to the moment of mourning my friend, however, I realized the loss of it, feeling a surge of anger that, frankly, threw me for the rest of the show. Post-show, I confronted Cyril, telling him that, while what had happened with his staff that afternoon was an innocent accident, his act of childishness was both mean-hearted and unprofessional. To his credit, he apologized, but reiterated his feelings of hurt about my callous treatment of his personal prop. Impasse. Although he later relented and gave me permission to use his staff, I refused. I'd find a way of using that moment to say goodbye to Portia, instead; in some ways it was more powerful and comprehensible than the rather laboured burial scene that I'd constructed prior to *Stick-Gate*. Petty? Pathetic? Puerile? That's what happens when a group of human beings spend so much intense, emotional time together, and in so vulnerable an environment.

An early reader of my draft manuscript for *Julius Caesar and Me* noted that I personally seemed to be oblivious to the obvious parallels that Brutus and Cassius have in their dysfunctional relationship. I think it's fair to say that the debrief argument is sharply demonstrated here. If only we could have resolved our differences in a calm and reasonable way. But, as explained earlier, once you're 'in role' it can be very hard to even recognize that you truly are borrowing from your character's state of mind. QED?

That incident, though hard at the time, proved to be the catalyst for a more respectful, professional and calm working relationship with Cyril. And all our resources of togetherness would be called upon when we finally got to the most exciting and high-pressured destination on this *Julius Caesar* Roadshow – Moscow.

16

Black *Caesar* in Russia

You may recall that in my late teens I had come across my first drama school by literally blindly picking out a name in *The Stage* newspaper. Studio '68 of Theatre Arts. I will always be grateful for the eighteen months I studied there before going on to LAMDA. Back in the early 1980s Studio '68's Principal Robert Henderson had introduced me to Russian theatre and I had been a fan ever since. Now, cut to thirty years later and I'm boarding a plane for Moscow with my wife, Manou, in tow, and a heart full of mixed feelings. Eastern Europeans have been given a rather bad press as far as foreign relations goes, especially when those foreigners are black. The football terraces of the East, where many of the cast and I were getting our views on Russian inclusivity from, are not, thankfully, the whole Eastern European world. There was some comfort to be had in that.

Not having visited an Eastern European city since Prague in 1989, I couldn't guess what would await this cast of black actors when we finally got to Moscow in November 2012. Shapkas were packed in the hope that we'd be warm enough and the cast braced themselves for a possibly chilly reception. It did feel a bit like we were going to do battle, silly as that sounds. But we were taking *Julius Caesar* to Russia, a country where a single leader had held sway for much of the past decade – a leader who had, in May of that year, made a triumphant comeback as Russian President; where Pussy Riot, an all-female, politically-focused, punk performance collective, had just been jailed for speaking out against the government and President Vladimir Putin. And here we were, about to perform a play about the assassination of a *dictator*, at the most prestigious of all the city's landmarks, the Moscow Art Theatre.

Customs took a little longer than expected and, without doubt, the ten-minute scrutiny my passport underwent felt inauspicious, compared to the thirty-second peremptory glance that my wife's French passport received. Relations with France were, at this point at least, more open and cordial than with Britain. Well, I hoped that was the reason and not the beginning of a hostile week in the wintry East.

I needn't have worried. The reception we received was exemplary and cordial. We felt welcomed by our hosts immediately and our accommodation in the heart of the capital was superb. Even the notoriously harsh Russian weather cooperated and we enjoyed temperatures well above freezing and, at times, in the high single digits for much of that week. The only incident that made me feel that I stood out merely for the colour of my skin happened in Red Square, on our first morning in Moscow. Manou and I had donned our shapkas and made our way to the most famous spot in the city. The looks I got walking along the street were motivated more by curiosity rather than hostility and – come on – I was a black man wearing a very furry shapka, so fair enough.

Arriving in Red Square, Manou and I did what everyone else was doing and took several shots of each other with the beautiful onion domes of St Basil's Cathedral in the background. While we were taking our pictures, I had noticed that several tourists were taking shots of something just behind us, so I shifted our position in order that they could get a better view. After moving out of the way three or four times, it then dawned on me that they were in fact trying to get a better view of me.

Now, I have had a few notable television appearances in my time and I'm confident that many of those programmes have been sold to Russia and elsewhere. However, my delusions of grandeur aside, that couldn't explain the paparazzi treatment. Then one man came up to me and, in improvised sign language, asked if he might take a picture with me. I wasn't sure if this was a good or a bad thing but he'd asked so politely that I felt I couldn't very well say no. He grinned away while his mother, or possibly his wife, took the shots. I managed to ask him where he was from and he proudly said, 'Romania!' He'd come a long way to see a black man.

So much for the tourist attraction that was Red Square. Perhaps, joking aside, the fact that I get stopped very occasionally for a picture with a fan in the UK made me less self-conscious and sensitive than the younger cast members. It certainly explains the thick skin I've developed about being stared at. An armour-plating that I didn't yet possess when I first went to New York with Manou in 1995 and we were stared at – often with open hostility – by folks of every ethnicity you can imagine. The Russian version was like water off a duck's back and I can honestly say that I did not encounter any overt hostility as a black man in the short, eventful, week we spent there. That isn't to say that other cast members were so lucky. The excellent young actor Jude Owusu, who played Cinna the Poet, both in our play and the exciting, interactive, monologue written by Tim Crouch, *I, Cinna,* was sorely offended when he was refused entry into a Moscow night club on the grounds that he was black. A filthy attitude that was not prevalent, but definitely present, in this city.

* * *

My first sight of the Moscow Art Theatre is a treasured memory. It was in the afternoon of that first day in Russia. I had turned the corner into

FIGURE 2 *The Moscow Art Theatre, Kamergersky Street.*
(Photo credit: Cyril Nri)

Kamergersky Street and noticed road works all down the side of a building.
It took me a while to figure out that behind the work's barriers was Anton
Chekov and Konstantin Stanislavski's famous theatre. It seemed so ordinary,
so simple, though beautiful for all that. It was also thrilling to see the posters
for *Julius Caesar* on the lampposts near the theatre.

I entered the building with a growing feeling of awe. It was as if, until this
point, I had not fully understood how massive a moment this was in my life
as an actor. The rehearsal period, the filming fortnight, the openings in
Stratford and London, followed by the tough tour, had helped to insulate me
from the momentousness of this event. But, when I saw the auditorium for
the first time, all that came into sharp focus at last and I truly felt that I was
living in a rarefied bubble of artistic bliss. *How did the boy from Willesden
Green get here?*

* * *

Stanislavski's theatre was opened in Moscow in 1898 and refurbished at the
turn of the twentieth century. Its look and feel was in stark contrast to the
lavish décor of the city's other famous venues, the Maly and Bolshoi
Theatres. In Stanislavski's time, those grand houses were state-run and

therefore under strict control. Having had the privilege that week to see a show at the Bolshoi, I was bowled over by its glittering gold and deep-red, lavish furnishings; its immense chandelier and monumental stage. It was a vast cavern of a space, that had forced the original theatre-managers into making the decision to present ballet and opera exclusively. This occurred

FIGURE 3 *Poster of* Julius Caesar *outside the Moscow Art Theatre.*
(Photo credit: Cyril Nri)

very soon after it was opened when everyone realized that its grandeur swamped any actor who stood on the stage.

Stanislavski and his fellow artistic director, Vladimir Nemirovich-Danchenko, decided that a new, stripped-back theatre should be inaugurated. Stanislavski's desire for naturalistic work and Nemirovich-Danchenko's love of literature combined, to form a powerful partnership with Anton Chekov's innovative, revolutionary and refreshingly naturalistic writing. The rest is history and the Moscow Art Theatre became the most famous theatre, not just in Russia, but throughout the theatrical world. The Stanislavski Method was adopted and adapted by teachers Lee Strasberg, Sanford Meisner, Stella Adler and many others in the United States. In turn, their methods were embraced by the best actors of the twentieth and twenty-first centuries: Montgomery Clift, James Dean, Marlon Brando, Daniel Day Lewis, Robert De Niro, Al Pacino, Marilyn Monroe, Meryl Streep, Jane Fonda . . . Stanislavski's influence on modern acting cannot be overstated and my generation is certainly indebted to him for our own eclectic take on his original methodology.

Stepping into the simple, pre-Art Deco interior of the Moscow Art Theatre was the actor's equivalent of entering Mecca. Honestly – it did feel like a sacred space. I am not overly sentimental about theatres and their histories, but this one really got to me. The simple wood panelling around the balcony walls, the flap-up wooden seating and the semi-circular, inclusive feel to the auditorium, all led me to realize that Stanislavski's desire was to eliminate any theatrical distractions and have the audience and actors all focused on one place – the stage. The most amazing moment of this first encounter was being shown the very seat where Stanislavski sat on rehearsal days. And there was his name on a small plaque: *Konstantin Sergeyevich Stanislavski*. Properly awe-inspiring.

But would the show really be worthy of the space we had now entered? Or was it, despite the fortnight's break, irredeemably knackered? The line run, a ritual refreshing of the play-text that takes place after a long interval between performances, would reveal much. This was to happen in the rehearsal rooms above the auditorium. Along the walls were the photographs of past Moscow Art Theatre actors, writers and directors. Many of them were unknown to us, but the few that I could decipher, in my faltering Cyrillic, were daunting enough: Maxim Gorky, Vselovod Meyerhold, Olga Knipper and the great Anton Chekov.

After an initial warm-up with the RSC's voice guru Lyn Darnley, we began our line run. There was a real quietness, a calm and a sense of reverence and care being taken with the text. Eye contact was strong and the characters re-emerged afresh. It seemed that the occasion was subduing any casual treatment of the words and that our sense of history was mastering any feelings of boredom we may have felt, despite the fact that we had now performed this play one hundred and thirty-eight times.

The historical impact of what we were undertaking was revealed to us the day before, in a press conference the likes of which I had never experienced in my, then, twenty-four-year career. A conference room in the hotel had been set aside for the event and the gathered press and accompanying cameras were impressive in their numbers. I have taken part in press junkets before, for various TV series and the odd feature film, but this was unique in my experience for a theatrical presentation. The room was packed and we, the panel, sat on a long table along the whole length of one wall. Greg and Jeremy Adams, our tour manager, were present, as were the lead actors: myself, Cyril, Jeffrey, Ray and Adjoa. Representatives from the Chekov Theatre Festival and the Moscow Art Theatre were with us, too, and they spoke passionately of the deeply rooted relationship that Russian theatre has always had with Shakespeare. He was, after all, one of the first playwrights to be performed at the Moscow Art Theatre when it was inaugurated at the end of the nineteenth century. What's more, we would be the first RSC company to have been to Moscow since Peter Hall's visit in 1968. The fact that we were an exclusively black company was not lost on anyone. Yet, that detail was definitely not what was exciting *us*. We felt that our excellence had made this possible. That feeling of confidence bled through the whole cast and affected our collective experience of the Moscow Art Theatre.

The questions in this press conference were very different from the usual, 'And how did you feel about working with Leonardo Di Caprio?'-type that I was used to from our own press. These questions, by contrast, ranged from, 'Is Africa uniquely suited to the telling of this story?' to 'Are you all Africans and do you all feel a strong connection to that continent?' followed by, 'Is suicide the best solution when one feels their political and ideological goals have been ultimately, and permanently, thwarted?' We all had to pause for thought before we answered that one. This specific, and forensic, line of questioning revealed a committed, respectful theatre tradition and gave us a sense of being taken seriously as thinking artists. Sadly, for us in the West, I haven't really experienced this depth of personal engagement with theatre anywhere else, except in Eastern Europe.

* * *

In the late winter of 1989, I was on tour with Declan Donnellan's Cheek by Jowl Theatre Company. We were presenting our production of Shakespeare's *The Tempest*, and one of our first venues was the National Theatre in Bucharest, Romania. As soon as we arrived in that city, we could palpably feel the oppressive atmosphere of a tightly reined-in populace – constantly watched, constantly insecure. We, in turn, were shadowed everywhere we went by a discreet chaperone – a middle-aged woman, who seemed more like someone's mother than a state spy. Small children, some as young as three or four, would approach us to sell us packets of cigarettes. We bought them happily, as we felt so sorry for them, but were soon told that giving them money only encouraged their 'bosses'. It turned out that these children were part of large, brutal, adult-led gangs and were treated appallingly by them. The country's negligent attitude to these strays has been well documented, but it was very moving to see them in the flesh. The shops were sadly empty, the food we ate bland and limited. Yet, we were pretty certain that we were getting the best that Western currencies could buy. How the ordinary people lived was beyond our comprehension.

Suitably humbled, we were then shown the theatre the day before our tech and first show. It proved a curious sight. In this 2,000-seat auditorium sat a curtained proscenium-arch, taking up much of the centre of the dress circle. When we asked what this strange, curtained structure signified, our theatre guide told us that it was, in fact, hiding just a few plush seats or thrones, made for the Romanian leader, Nicolae Ceausescu. He had dreamt of a visit by the former Soviet General Secretary Leonid Brezhnev in the 1960s, and had built this theatre-within-the-theatre accordingly. That hoped-for visit never took place, but the useless structure remained. A mirror of the dictator Ceausescu's lavish palace – a monstrously excessive monument to waste and decadent ostentation. Meanwhile, in the streets, children begged and starved in oppressive circumstances. The scene was set for a somewhat tense first night, as we noticed all the politburo 'suits' sitting in the first few rows, while all the students occupied the circle. It was in this electric atmosphere that we began the play.

Declan's conceit for *The Tempest* was to imagine that Prospero was an actor-manager who had hired a group of seemingly random actors, to play various roles in a devised play. He chose me first, with the opening line of *The Tempest* – 'Boatswain!' – and I immediately jumped on to a large straw chest, miming the movements of turning a huge ship's wheel. My lines were then said in a Jamaican accent, with a few judicious alterations to the text thrown in by me, 'Here, Master. Ah wha' de cheer?' And off we went, with various actors being picked out for Miranda, Ferdinand, Caliban, etc. We went through the play with little or no sound coming from the auditorium; we had no idea whether there was comprehension or horror at what we were doing with this precious play. But Cheek by Jowl were known for turning Shakespeare and our pre-conceived notions of how he should be done very firmly, sometimes violently, on their head. There were plenty of moments that had met with confusion and even anger while we had been on the road in the UK.

In Act 4 Scene 1, Prospero evokes a masque to consecrate the love vows between his daughter Miranda and her lover Ferdinand. In this sequence, the gods Juno, Iris and Ceres dance, calling on the spirits of the island to celebrate the love match. In our version, Prospero/Actor-Manager left the stage and the actors, dressed pretty scantily as the various Bacchanalian deities, would go crazy with freedom; launching into an 'acid house' rave sequence. Acid House raves – i.e. impromptu parties where young people listened to pulsing electronic music and took drugs, such as acid or ecstasy – were all the rage in the UK at that time. We would, rather embarrassedly, perform in our tutus and strange, Bacchic costumes, a version of a rave; complete with strobing lights, a drum kit, a saxophone and shouts of 'Aceeeed! Aceeeed!' I say embarrassedly because not many of us during our previous leg of the tour in the UK thought that the people of Cambridge, Bury St Edmunds, Winchester or Bracknell really knew what we were portraying. After about thirty seconds of this craziness we would chant, 'Freedom, freedom', until, mercifully, Prospero returned and halted our fun. Then the strobing lights would stop and the play would begin again. Polite applause, oftentimes sheer bewilderment, met us for the most part in the UK after this sequence and we always approached it feeling like we'd be glad when it was over with. Though, I have to admit, it was also fun. I've always liked that sense of the audience being a bit unsure of what they are supposed to make of what they're seeing. It adds a frisson of tension to our work.

But, here we were, in a country that had not been allowed much modern pop, or disco. And we were trying to connect them with what was then the most current wave of music amongst British youth, Acid House. Hopeless, we would have all said beforehand. And we would have been right about that – the students had little or no experience of this type of music, let alone this particular dance craze. Remember, this was way before the Internet, before Twitter and YouTube; before social networks meant that young people anywhere in the world, with access to the right technology, could connect with every youth movement on a global level, at the touch of a button. But, despite their obvious puzzlement about the music, when we finally got to shouting, 'Freedom, freedom . . .' the roof blew off the place. We noticed that the 'suits' in the front row were craning their necks over their shoulders, to look up at the balcony behind them. In the dress circle, on either side of that monstrosity of a proscenium-arch, the students had all stood up and were stretching their arms out over the balcony, screaming in unison, '*FREEDOM, FREEDOM!*' We were astonished and powerless, at that moment. Though we had, in effect, run out of music, they continued shouting from their souls. Eventually, the actor playing Prospero, Timothy Walker, stepped on to the stage and the students quietened down. Prospero's first line at this point is, 'Well done! Avoid; no more.'

Bloody powerful stuff; and I have never viewed theatre in the same way since. It can be fun, it can be frivolous, but it can also set a fire under the cauldron of history. Not that we had much to do with the coming revolution, of course, but we certainly felt the latent power of the force of political momentum that led to the eventual end of the oppressive Ceausescu regime. On the sixteenth of December of that year, the revolt finally broke out and forty-two years of draconian communism ended in that country. The same crowd reaction was repeated in former Czechoslovakia, when we performed at their beautiful national theatre in Prague. Shakespeare, a catalyst for revolution? Am I guilty of giving too much credit to the communal, transformative power of relevant theatre?

* * *

After our sober, heartfelt line run of *Julius Caesar* and the deeply contemplative press conference, we were all rightly fired-up to give our very best to this short week of intense theatre. And it definitely started with a bang.

The tech was smooth and easy from the actor's point of view and our dress rehearsal uneventful. Quick changes and entrances had been worked out; the space made safe for all the running to and fro backstage that the show entailed. On the first night, we were pretty much cruising in our usual controlled way and had reached Act 4 Scene 2 and the beginning of the Tent Scene – the pivotal scene of the second half of the play, when Brutus childishly goads Cassius to the point of his attempted suicide. The overhead sur-titles seemed to be working well. The audience were clearly not needing to glance too much at the Russian translation above. So far, so brilliant, I thought. And to have the captions out of the way of the performer's vision and out of the way of the stage lighting was a masterstroke that I wish dramatic theatre would steal from the world of opera. Every appropriately configured theatre that can afford it should adopt this placement.

Cyril and I were on a roll and the emotional charge of the scene was palpable. I doubted if it had gone as well as this since Stratford; honest, powerful and full of vulnerability. The space had affected us all; our playing was truthful and not pushed. The spirit of Stanislavski was present in the very architecture of the stage and auditorium. If I pushed too hard vocally, it almost seemed to whisper a gentle but firm, 'Shh'. If I wandered around the stage, it called out for more stillness and specificity. It was like acting under a huge magnifying glass, where every gesture, every reaction, seemed to be exaggerated by the space. A throwback to my first experience of a theatrical space; in my school assembly hall during *Oliver!*. Like that hall in Willesden Green, this space seemed to hold its breath collectively. Less was definitely more here.

Then came the moment when Cassius is attempting to guide the hand of Brutus to stab him. I allowed Cyril to grab my hand as usual and he pulled the knife toward him while I pulled it away. Apart from the weeks of training we had undergone with the RSC's clever, resourceful and creative fight director, Kevin McCurdy, we had gone through this intense sequence of moves at least a hundred and forty times in front of an audience; not counting the many, many times we had covered it through fight calls (a pre-show warm-up of all the combat moments in the play) and on set during the filming fortnight. It was always safe and there had never been a problem with it. Only once, in that whole time, had we even had what might be termed a minor incident. That occurred one night in Stratford, when we both let the dagger fall and it landed on its sharp point, embedding itself in the stage. Dramatic, but perfectly safe. Therefore, we were caught unawares by this familiar moment. Because this time, something went terribly wrong. As Cyril grabbed my hand and pulled it toward his stomach, I lost control of the dagger momentarily and the force of his grab took the dagger out of both of our hands, as it flew, in a slow and graceful arc, into the auditorium. We were both shocked and, briefly, froze. I moved forward to the edge of the stage and said in English, of course, 'Sorry, ladies and gentlemen, I think we should stop.' Cyril reiterated this and I knelt down at the edge of the stage to see where the dagger had gone. To my horror, I saw immediately what had happened to it.

The arc of the surprisingly heavy weapon had taken it on to the apron of the stage. It had then skimmed on the black felt on the edge of the apron, sliding straight into the face of a lady sitting in the front row. By the time I reached her, her companion had placed the dagger on to the stage and the woman was holding her face. Petrified of what I would find, I very gently pulled her hand away to see what damage we had done. As far as I could see in the relatively dark auditorium, the side of her nose had a tiny red mark, but she was otherwise unscathed. A massive wave of relief hit me and I asked her companion to take her out for treatment. All this in English and broad gestures, naturally. It turned out, in the end, that she was not too badly hurt at all – just understandably shocked.

As I climbed back onstage, Suzy Bourke, our stage manager, was ushering a translator on, who explained to the audience that we were going to take a short break and would resume once the captions had been reset. Just before exiting, however, I began to wrack my brains over a Russian word that my wife had gotten up the previous night to search for. It had been bugging her so much that she had switched on the light in our hotel room and grabbed our little translation book. I remember tetchily reminding her that I was opening a show the next night and would she 'please, give it a rest'. Now it came back to me, and I was very grateful for Manou's persistence. I turned to face the auditorium and, taking a deep breath, said what sounded like, '*Izvinitsye*', which was as close as I could get to 'I'm sorry'. The audience, to my great surprise and relief, actually applauded my feeble attempt at a Russian apology and we left the stage.

Everyone was huddled around the prompt corner entrance, not knowing whether we were going to have to wait five, ten or fifteen minutes before we could go on. The caption controller was having difficulty finding the right spot in the Russian translation that corresponded with where we would be restarting the scene. I looked at Cyril and realized that he was thinking the same thing as I was. Any moment we would be asked to restart the show from the suicide attempt and the struggle with the dagger. I think we both feared we would lose our concentration, with all the chatter and speculation that was surrounding us. Without speaking about it, just by a kind of instinct, we quickly took ourselves away from the crowd and

FIGURE 4 *The auditorium of the Moscow Art Theatre during a post-show Q&A.*
(Photo credit: Cyril Nri)

FIGURE 5 *Some of the* Julius Caesar *cast and crew outside the Moscow Art*
Theatre.
(Photo credit: Cyril Nri)

somehow found ourselves kneeling in the shadow of the upstage blackout curtains, hands clasped in solidarity, and re-focusing ourselves on where we had gotten to in the story. As Cyril has since said of this incident, it was the most effecting moment he has ever had onstage. And I cannot but agree. It was a beautiful expression of reconciliation. I thank whatever Stanislavskian spirit was in the theatre that day for bringing us back to ourselves again – connected, empathetic and solid. We've been firm friends, brothers, ever since. It was a fantastic way to be 'live' in the theatre of my hero Konstantin Stanislavski and a brilliant way to reboot *Julius* for the coming adventures.

Apart from Caesar and Portia, shouting at a member of the audience who was taking pictures during the show on the following night, the rest of the week was wonderfully uneventful and satisfying. The applause was the best we had ever had. Hearing shouts of 'Bravo' echoing around the auditorium, seeing a mass standing ovation and a rush to the front of the stage to throw flowers to us, will live with me as long as my memory holds out.

Our little *Julius Caesar* that had started life in the rehearsal room on Cato Road in Clapham eighteen months before – or more properly, in Nelson Mandela's cell on Robben Island in December 1977 – was triumphant in, arguably, the most important and prestigious theatre in modern theatrical history.

New York, that other theatrical superpower, was to follow, after a four-month hiatus.

17

Brooklyn Bound

Much of what I'd been through so far with *Julius Caesar* was a mirror of previous theatre experiences. The difference being that this time it was simultaneously harder and better than before. Harder, because it was a much longer stint on one show than I had ever experienced. Better, because the rewards and variety of this journey were much greater than I could have hoped for. Particularly when I think of the dark times that the regional tour had brought. The time in Stratford was saner and more creatively satisfying than my first visit twenty years before. My Eastern European adventures bore more fruit in terms of my rekindled love for the craft than I could possibly have foreseen. New York was, hopefully, going to be a repeat performance of my earlier, electrifying *Hamlet* experience.

Hamlet: the play that took me for the first time to New York, starred Ralph Fiennes, Tara Fitzgerald, Francesca Annis and a very young Damian Lewis. I was newly married and starry-eyed in many ways. Ralph's profile was rapidly increasing and the guests we received on a daily basis backstage at the Belasco Theatre, in Broadway's theatre district, were stellar. Kirk Douglas, Laurence Fishburne, Cher, Harrison Ford, Angela Basset, Tom Hanks, the late, great Lauren Bacall, Gwyneth Paltrow and her then partner, Brad Pitt and many, many others. It was impossible not to feel the thrill of bearing witness to this wave of Hollywood glamour. I will never forget watching Ralph negotiate the hordes of autograph hunters behind metal barriers, crowding the stage door exit every night. There were bodyguards and a waiting limo for him each evening. We were all caught up in the whirlwind of this exhilarating time.

Though I was only eight years out of drama school at that point, I remember cautioning the younger cast members like Rupert Penry-Jones and Damian Lewis not to expect experiences like this one every time they did a play – whether that play went to New York or not. I'm sure they felt terribly patronized, and not surprisingly. Both those actors have had full and brilliant careers since those early days. I still maintain that it was good advice, though, and I know from my subsequent experiences that having a British production on Broadway is as rare for most actors as stardust. Although *Julius Caesar* would not be performed on Broadway, we were going to be playing in one of the most exciting and vibrant theatres New York has to offer and one of its oldest: the Brooklyn Academy of Music (BAM).

BAM opened its doors on Montague Street, Brooklyn Heights, in 1861. Amongst the performers in those first years were Ellen Terry, Edwin Booth and Tomas Salvini. That exalted tradition continued into the twentieth century with readings and recitals by Booker T. Washington, an early African American leader of the civil rights movement; Paul Robeson, black mega-star of the 1920s, 1930s and 1940s; and President Franklin Delano Roosevelt. The new building on Lafayette Street, Brooklyn, its present home, was opened early in the twentieth century and BAM continued with its sister buildings, The Fisher and The Harvey, to welcome such esteemed international artists as Peter Brook, Pina Bausch, Rudolph Nureyev, Paul Simon, Merce Cunningham, Philip Glass, the Royal National Theatre, Kirov Opera, Chuck Davis, Bill T. Jones and Robert Lepage. And I haven't even scratched the surface of the host of artists from every corner of the globe that make up its usual classy diet.

While all this international activity is impressive enough, the dazzling array of artists do not distract BAM from what seems to be its main thrust: art in the community. And the specific community that surrounds these glorious buildings is the largest Afro-Caribbean community in New York. It was delicious to know that we were here under the banner of 'international artists' and would be rubbing shoulders with the great and the good of black America, as well as living amongst the vibrant and powerfully creative locals. What better place could there be for an African *Julius Caesar* than here, in the heart of New York's coolest neighbourhood? We couldn't wait to see how we would go down.

Our guide in all things BAM was Stacey Dinner, liaison between the institution and the actors – a knowledgeable, bubbly lady who was keen to show us a great time in her home city. The reception, held at our hotel, was lavish and generous. Afterwards, I took a walk around the neighbourhood of the Adams Street Courthouse, feeling safe and at ease. Conveniently, our hotel was about a mile from the theatre, so the walk to the Harvey Theatre was always a pleasant one. Walking the streets around that area felt familiar, as if I were in Brixton, south London. The sounds and smells of Caribbean music and food, and the energy of the people going about their daily lives, made us all feel perfectly at home. In contrast to much of Manhattan, Brooklyn's residents are a very mixed bag and from one neighbourhood to another the atmosphere and cultural mix can change dramatically.

On our first evening off, we were invited to see the RSC's other production, *Matilda*; recently opened to rave reviews on Broadway. We were sensing that this was going to be a very important moment in RSC history and that further heightened our excitement. Crossing Brooklyn Bridge in a taxi that night after seeing *Matilda*, I could only hope our *Julius Caesar* would receive half the plaudits of that sold-out musical. The work needed to ensure just such a positive reception would start the next day.

* * *

The Harvey Theatre is a beautifully rough space. Inaugurated with Peter Brook's production of *The Mahabharata* in 1987, it was designed along the same lines as Brook's Parisian theatre, La Bouffe Du Nord. It features rough-worked walls with the plaster stripped back, wooden seating and an auditorium that wraps around the action on the flat stage. Our set fit the style of the building perfectly and Michael Vale was bowled over by how much his design was mirrored and complemented by the space; with its Romanesque columns flanking both ends of the stalls, topped by the broken capitols, reaching up into the gods. We couldn't have found a better penultimate home for our journey with *Julius Caesar*. Penultimate because our final destination was to be the Southern Theatre in Columbus, Ohio. That struck me as a bit of a looming anti-climax to our tour, to be perfectly honest, so I was determined to enjoy every moment of this New York sojourn.

I ran the length of the bay near Brooklyn Heights in the mornings, being treated to early morning sun for the most part and unseasonably warm April weather. The stunning views of Manhattan across the water and the massive edifices of the Brooklyn and Manhattan Bridges were a tonic to the jet-lagged soul each day. Our three-week stay was going to be a lot of fun, I reckoned, and I was also heartened by the fact that we were not going to be on tour for the twelve weeks that had been originally mooted. I'd baulked a bit at the idea because, as I've said, taking time away from home was bad enough, but extending that time to include a further three months on the road was almost more than my family could bear. They'd also suffered through the disappointment of the false hope that I would be leaving the production earlier. It had been tough missing each other for so long, so the three weeks in Brooklyn, and the subsequent week in Ohio, felt like an ideal way to finish off this marathon run.

To my great relief, our first night went well, as did the press night. Our reviews, particularly from feared *New York Times* critic Ben Brantley, were enthusiastic and complimentary. Good reviews make life easier for the box office, naturally, and lend any production an energy that can get it through the toughest of times. We were going to need every ounce of encouragement, too, as the punishing schedule that BAM and the RSC put us through began to take its toll; cast member Marcus Griffiths being an exhausted casualty of that. On top of this, we were all disappointed that the make up of the audiences was simply not reflective of the local neighbourhood.

When I got back home I wrote to Mary Reilly, Director of Artists Services at BAM, about the issue of scheduling and also the dearth of black faces in the audience for our Brooklyn run. Mary Reilly's reply came a few weeks later and gave me much comfort. Mary was kind enough to pass on my concerns and I was deeply impressed by her swift and genuinely positive response.

It is very rare for an institution as vast and prestigious as BAM to reply in the affirmative to a complaint about their practices. To BAM's great credit, when I returned there to perform my monologue *Sancho – An Act of Remembrance* in 2015, I was welcomed with open arms. Many workshops and discussions with the multi-ethnic staff were organized. We debated in various gatherings the issues surrounding the unfortunate elitist feel that BAM, and mainstream theatre in general, suffers under. The full and frank 'Town Hall' meeting on reaching out more effectively to the diverse communities around them was tackled bravely and with a refreshing honesty. I have never experienced so thorough and so public a self-examination by any large arts organization in my life. So, hats off to them.

* * *

I was greatly stimulated by two events in particular during this three-week New York run. On the first night, we had a reception laid on for the sponsors and supporters of BAM. When all the speeches were over and the champagne glasses had been raised, I stole over to the bar for a bottle of local ale. While there, I bumped into a man who bore a striking resemblance to the young Albert Einstein. I greeted him and when he replied I smiled to myself – his accent sounded a lot like the one I imagined Einstein to have had. I couldn't help myself and said, 'Do you know, you really look like Albert Einstein? What line of work are you in?' He smiled affably and told me that his name was Ivan Bodis-Wollner and that he was professor of neurology at SUNY Downstate Medical Centre in Brooklyn. He then said, 'I have to confess to being very surprised at your performance'. Here we go, I thought. Another compliment about my *Welsh* Brutus. He went on to say, 'I was first of all struck by the fact that the Brutus of the second half was an almost completely different character to the Brutus in the first.' Now, this might seem like a barbed comment, but I was gratified. My attempts at creating a Brutus who reacted to his given circumstances scene by scene and even within each scene, were obviously working. He then made this observation: 'You also shocked me when you came out for the curtain call. This man, that we had seen so broken and alone, taking his own life and at his lowest ebb, comes bouncing, yes, bouncing back from the dead and gleefully took his bow. I was left wondering how he did that.' We laughed and I said, 'It's strange you should say that, because I've been trying to debrief from my characters for years and you're the first person to have noticed the change in so scientific a way.' 'Ah, debrief!', he said, his eyes widening. 'Tell me more about that. What does that mean to you . . .?' I almost felt like I was on Doctor Freud's couch, what with the way he looked and that accent.

I explained tentatively the way I had come by the technique via my two counsellor friends and the fact that it had helped me slough off the emotions of the characters I portrayed. His next observation had me floored, and that feeling you sometimes get when your whole skin around your neck and scalp starts to tingle with excitement came over me. 'I once had a friend in Bulgaria, where I grew up, who became an actor, and he was brilliant. One day, my mother and I went to see him perform a great role, as a famous general. When we met him afterwards and went out for supper, I was astonished to see that he dressed a little like the general he had just played and, what's more, was talking and behaving like him for much of our evening together. After some hours, the "general" receded and I could talk to my friend again. It was an act of debriefing that I could see happening before my very eyes.'

Fascinated, I then asked Ivan if he felt the idea that an actor could be so taken up in the story that he loses part of himself, was myth or truth? And, if it *was* true, then did it also follow (as I had begun to suspect) that the audience performed a similar – though less intense – feat when seeing a performance onstage? Do they sit there, sometimes having been reluctantly dragged to the theatre, with their week's emotional baggage in their hands and then see, for instance, a man mourning his father's death and his mother marrying his father's brother? And does that audience member then slowly put down his bags, forget his own troubles and invest, wholeheartedly, in this stranger's concerns? Is *that* myth or truth? Ivan's enthusiastic reply was that it was indeed a scientifically observed phenomenon. Neuroscience has identified a specific neuron in the brain which is activated when one human being desires to empathize with another. It is sometimes – not altogether accurately – called the mirror neuron and was first observed in monkeys. When the keeper scratches his head, the monkey does likewise; when the keeper taps his chin, the monkey follows suit. The phrase 'monkey-see, monkey-do' comes to mind. It may well have its origin in an observation that was made a long time ago, before scientists were able to study the brain in such fine detail and confirm the existence of this evolutionary neural component. A survival technique, no less, that helped us evolve as a communal species through the imitation of tested, safe behaviours. I was blown away and really touched by this enlightening and profoundly engaging conversation. I hope to talk more about this phenomenon with Ivan in the future.

For now, I absolutely believe that my observations on the altruistic nature of the audience – their need to empathize in order to leave their cares behind for a moment – their compulsion to connect with their own humanity, is real and powerful.

*　*　*

My other encounter was less personal but no less enlightening for all that. James Shapiro, Professor of English and Comparative Literature at Columbia

University, had arranged for a small audience to see extracts of *Julius Caesar* and listen to his scholarly insights on the history of the play in performance. It was to be a thrilling evening full of illumination and surprises, even for those cast members present who had been living with the play for well over a year.

James introduced Cyril and me and we played out the first Cassius/Brutus exchange for the audience of about one hundred and fifty people. After this, he asked about our thoughts on this initial conversation involving the two protagonists. We responded to his questions, then got to play the scene through again. It was great for the audience to have the play broken down like this, as they were then able to see the very scenes mentioned played out in front of them. A lively, interactive method for getting inside this play. James fired many pertinent questions at us, asking about our character's motivations and whether Brutus, in particular, felt manipulated by Cassius. It was great to be able to answer for Brutus in a more informed and objective way than I would have been able to way back in rehearsals. The major difference between what I would have said then and what I said when James asked that key question about Brutus' mind-set, was the year's journey that I had gone through with this complex and fascinating character.

For instance, I had begun the rehearsal process feeling sure that Brutus entered into the conspiracy as an unadulterated act of altruistic generosity, toward the people of Rome. Wholly pure in his intentions and without an ounce of pride or arrogance. All that changed during rehearsals, as I explored in fine detail his words and actions from scene to scene. And on top of these on-the-ground observations, I also had the opportunity to take an historical step back from the canvas and focus on what the bigger picture might tell us. That opportunity had come during the second spell of rehearsals after our filming fortnight.

I was invited by the British Museum to take part in their ground-breaking Shakespeare exhibition. This monumental display was to be housed in one of their main galleries and would consist of artefacts, *objets d'art* and various domestic items from around the world, inspired in one way or another by Shakespeare's canon. There were manuscripts from early editions of the plays, a sample of writing that might have been in Shakespeare's own hand and glove-maker's implements from his day – perhaps exactly the same kind used by his father in his Stratford workshop. While all of these objects were fascinating in themselves, none were more resonant than the *Robben Island Bible*, displayed in a glass case and opened at the very page annotated by Nelson Mandela in 1977. It was a wonderful exhibition and it remains a highlight of the time I spent with *Julius Caesar*.

My particular task for the British Museum exhibition was to be part of an installation featuring actors filmed reciting extracts from Shakespeare's plays. Brutus' speech to the crowd post-assassination was chosen and, to add spice to the pot, I was given a coin as a prop which had been found in Greece dating from the time of Brutus' exile from Rome. This tiny object helped me a great deal because it answered a burning question I had about Brutus. A question that no amount of research had so far managed to answer. Was Brutus *ashamed* or *proud* of his actions on the ides of March? It may seem obvious from the outside, but so much of what he says and does as a character from moment to moment leaves room for uncertainty. His refusal to be gung-ho about killing Antony, his hatred of the sin of Caesar but not the sinner, Caesar, his angst when alone and with Portia. All these led me to believe that he was carrying a burden of guilt about the act of killing his 'Chief'. However, one look at this coin, minted in Brutus' time and pierced through so that it may be worn as a medallion on a chain, altered and enriched my opinion of him forever.

On the obverse is a depiction of Brutus with the inscription *'Brutus Imperator'*. Roughly translated: Brutus the Conqueror. On the reverse was a freedman's cap, centre, with two daggers on either side of it and the inscription *'The Ides of March'*. The minting of this coin by Brutus could only mean one thing. Far from being ashamed of his actions on that momentous March day, he was extremely proud of them. Clearly, his motivations were not solely his desire for the people to be free as shown by the presence – of all things – of a freedman's cap, but also for personal glory (*'Brutus Imperator'*). He must surely have felt that he had freed his people from the yoke of a selfishly ambitious dictator and had, therefore, legitimately earned the right to be called Conqueror. These insights changed fundamentally any shame-driven views I had on Brutus' involvement in Caesar's assassination. It altered permanently my playing of all the scenes from the Orchard/Conspiracy Scene onwards. It's also a forceful condemnation of the attitude that there's no need for research one often hears from some artists. I think we short-change our intelligence in this ostrich approach to the work we're given and risk robbing the audience of insights that our detailed research may have thrown up. Actors should always try to illuminate the work they are involved in and keeping themselves in the dark about facts surrounding the characters and situations in the works they perform cannot add to this illumination. Instinct takes us only so far, but – combined with knowledge – it can truly lead to powerful and original work. Attempting to be specific for each character and understanding their choices is what any good actor seeks. Research is one of our major tools and, honestly, it's enriching and fun.

A mini-example of this was at drama school. I had been given the part of Bottom the Weaver in Shakespeare's *A Midsummer Night's Dream*. I could tell it was a funny role, of course, but it seemed to me that there must have been a reason why Shakespeare chose the name 'Bottom', for his main comedic character. Apart from the obvious toilet-humour in the name itself, I thought the word worth exploring. What I found was a striking definition. Bottom: a skein of yarn. The description was of a round ball of thread used by weavers! Brilliant, I thought, I'll ask to have a fat suit made. My roly-poly Bottom got a lot of laughs. No doubt, these days, I may have been deterred from this 'funny

FIGURE 6 *Photograph of Paterson Joseph standing below the British Museum Shakespeare exhibit of him holding the 'Brutus Coin', 2012. (Credit: © The Trustees of the British Museum)*

fat man' act, but it worked. And I can't believe that William, whose father John Shakespeare was a glove maker and who would have known very well what a 'bottom' was, could have passed up the opportunity of turning our idea of the lover upside down. From the typical slender youth to this round ball of a man. I've believed in investigating hidden gems ever since.

And so, my gratitude to Henry Flynn, curator of coins and medals at the British Museum for that one in particular (a.k.a. 'The Coin-Wrangler' on any film set he's on). Thanks to Henry, my answers to James Shapiro's questions were bled through with insider knowledge. Brutus was proud of his actions and brooked no apologies for them.

During this wonderful evening, James Shapiro offered us and the audience present a brilliant breakdown of everything that we tried to get into our production – ideas of morality versus political expediency; contrasts in goals and routes to those goals; hot, indignant anger versus cold, righteous/self-righteous choices. All of these themes are contained within *Julius Caesar*. Shapiro helped us to see the play and its protagonists in more intricate detail than anyone had managed to before now. We were one year into the journey and still there was more to be mined in this short, powerful play.

* * *

New York came to an end with an exhausted cast just about ready to wind down and go home. However, we had one more week to go. We were to end our *Julius Caesar* marathon in Columbus, Ohio. Our connection to this city was tenuous, it seemed, to most of us before we got there. We were leaving this vibrant, African American community and, knackered though we were, were being asked to go to a largely white, conservative (as we saw it) backwater in order to show willing for our sponsors, Ohio State University. They had apparently supplied a hefty amount of cash to enable us to make this trip, so we were clearly duty-bound to give them a week of the show. This was going to be the last but least, the straw that would break the camel's back and various other clichés of defeated fatigue. An anti-climax, if ever there was one. Well – not for the first time in this story – I couldn't have been more wrong.

First of all, our reception in Ohio, at the sponsor's welcome party, bore all the hallmarks of genuine, American hospitality. Our accommodation was quiet and central, without being in the party quarter of town. It was a beautiful, bright, late-spring evening when I left the hotel behind and strolled across the road to find a place to walk. Soon, I stumbled upon the Scioto River. A long, winding stretch of water cutting through the city and rolling on for miles through quiet country walkways. Like a River Avon, American style. Over the next week, I would walk, or run, both banks of this wide tributary, sloughing off the last year's tension and exhaustion. The cleanliness of the place, the quietness and general friendliness of this city were the antidote to the frenetic, constantly stimulating, New York City. Here, I felt that I'd finally found America – a place of contrasts, where aggression was low and the main aim of its citizens seemed to be to live as calmly and respectfully with the folks around them as possible. I could see why this place was a favourite stop-off for President Obama on numerous occasions and why he had planned to speak at the University while we were there. The fact that Ohio was one of the main states that supported his presidency must have helped, too. I could understand why those travelling on Harriet Tubman's underground railroad – ferrying African American slaves from the brutal plantations in the southern United States, to the relative freedom of the northern states – had felt themselves safe once they'd reached this spot. It was a haven in the true sense of the word.

* * *

There's some confusion about middle-America in Europe, in supposing that middle-America is like middle-England or the French *profonde*. Isolated, remote, insular and racist. There are similarities, but the sense of identity is not the same, the racial mix is not the same and the opportunity for anyone – from any background – to rise to the top of political, business and artistic life is not the same. Racism – vicious, murderous and callous – has always existed in America. A complex web of guilt, fear and anger leads US race relations and it is far from a paradise for immigrants. However, despite these tensions, America voted a black man into the White House – twice. By contrast, the rigid European class and ethnic structures make it incredibly difficult for anyone not born into a privileged position to rise to the top in areas of great influence. In my opinion, our restrictive ethnicity-based cultures, rooted in large part on a long-standing and false assumption that white Europeans are superior to other ethnic groups that find themselves here, has stunted the growth of society in Europe generally and within artistic and political life specifically. My early school life, discussed in Chapter One, is a mirror of precisely that kind of oppressive, patronizing thinking.

The recent BBC television documentary, *Will Britain Ever Have a Black Prime Minister?* presents the true, statistical facts of academic life for black British children in the UK. The programme details how black children are often singled out as being trouble when they may only be boisterous; thick, when they may be simply struggling with bilingualism. Shockingly, the streaming of kids begins at nursery school. Children as young as three or four are being excluded from playgroups and nurseries on the grounds that they are disruptive and out of control. This kind of over-reaction to the naughty behaviour of black pupils is seen at all levels of state school education. The system of fast-track exclusions, suspensions and expulsions has led to a catastrophic situation where the majority of young black people in the UK will end up with a much poorer education than their white and Asian counterparts. Not coincidentally, a large proportion of the prison population includes people who are well below-par in terms of academic achievement. Ignorance, coupled with hostility towards the authorities that have let you down, together with the poverty that usually accompanies these conditions, are a lethal cocktail of social, economic and mental handicaps. We can talk about people pulling themselves up by their bootstraps but surely you have to be given a pair of boots to begin with? What an awful, hampered start for these British children.

Actor David Harewood, who presents the *Black Prime Minister* documentary, shocked me when he noted that black pupils' work is often marked down in school simply because the teacher knows them to be black. Clearly, even if this is happening in isolated cases, it is an horrific fact. Sadly, the cases highlighted in this excellent programme are far from exceptional. David added that it is only when these black pupils are in the anonymized exam system – where their ethnicity is largely hidden – that their results markedly improve. No longer subject to ethnic prejudice, no longer out-of-place in the system and their intrinsic, untapped, potential gets a chance to shine through. Despite all the previous obstacles, they achieve higher grades, go on to decent employment and the very real chance of a good, stable, fulfilled life. It's worth repeating that there remains a solid correlation between a poor education, poverty and crime.

Further, this blindness to the merits of non-Eurocentric expression is most starkly seen in our art galleries and on our opera and ballet stages. Where black people have made inroads in the area of art it has been hard won. Constantly having to prove oneself worthy of equal consideration is the exhausting inheritance of years of externally imposed limitations and presumptions of white European supremacy. Notions of superiority stem from an inbred national insecurity, however. An irrational fear of losing oneself, one's identity, in embracing the foreign and the unknown. A notion of superiority, then, that is manifestly untrue and, therefore, in the often unconscious logic of the deluded, imperative that it be reinforced with an even more extreme form of nationalistic pride.

American identity, by contrast, is born out of their history – imperfect though it is and freighted with myth – that tells them very clearly they are all johnny-come-latelies to American shores. From the earliest European explorers, to the English Pilgrim Fathers and thence to all the other nations whose people flowed into Ellis Island, Americans have always started from scratch – building their culture from the fragments of what they rescued from their original nations. The notable exceptions to this historical truth are Native Americans who, while they have been only relatively recently acknowledged for who they are – the First Americans – remain an undenied and undeniable part of the heritage of that country. There is an enviable openness and availability of opportunity in the US that is sadly lacking in Europe and, therefore, the idea of giving everyone an equal chance at success in artistic, political and business life in Europe remains, for the moment at least, an ideal that has still to be tried and tested.

Thanks, in large part, to the success of this *Julius Caesar* tour, I have just started working in America after being rather reluctant to embrace the Hollywood market. The opportunities this has afforded me as a black man have been a major catalyst for that change of heart. America, and its troubled racial history, is a model of a still relatively young nation trying to find its identity. That struggle is fascinating to us in the UK as, frequently, what happens in America is followed globally by other countries, eventually. I firmly believe that, if the opportunities to rise through merit in the US could be mirrored in the UK, our ethnic minority youth would be moving into positions of national influence a lot faster than they currently are.

* * *

Ohio surprised the *Julius Caesar* company because it was here we were finally given the specific kind of welcome we thought the play might have received elsewhere. The mayor of Columbus, Michael B. Coleman, an African-American who looks like a cross between movie actors Billy D. Williams and Clark Gable, organized events at which, surprisingly, we actors were given room to speak. That might sound like a no-brainer – hearing from the people who have just performed for you – but this is one of the frustrations for actors at many corporate events. Folks in suits, who haven't broken into even a mild sweat all evening, take the plaudits for having written the cheques. Fair enough, I guess, as we wouldn't even be there without them. But, in Ohio, our 'Movie Star Mayor' was happy to let us speak. On one such occasion, I recalled a childhood memory that I was spontaneously able to share with the gathered guests.

> Though we are close now, when I was growing up, my father had been a bit of a distant presence, particularly when it came to Christmas and birthdays. Some people just don't like these occasions, I guess, or they invoke bad memories for them. Who can say in my dad's case? So, the three times he gave me a gift, stand out in my memory. The first was a pair of sunglasses he bought for me when I was seven, after he had noticed my squinting grimace in a photograph taken at a christening in the summer. I was so proud of those cool (though short-lived) glasses and can remember their shiny, dark brown rims vividly. The second gift from Dad was a small guitar. I would have been about eight years old then. But, though he could get a decent tune out of it, Dad neglected to teach me how to play it. Shame, but I was mightily pleased to have a guitar. And finally, when I was ten, my dad took me shopping one Christmas and asked me to pick out one thing I wanted. For some reason, I chose a light-blue sweatshirt with – of all things – Ohio State University, emblazoned boldly on it. I cherished that sweatshirt in the same way that I had loved the other two rare offerings from my dad and perhaps even more because I wore it until I could barely get it over my head. And now, here I was in that very place printed on my favourite sweater.

The crowd thought this was hilarious.

Actually, I felt quite moved by the memory and became determined to go to Ohio State University (OSU) to check out their souvenir shop. I did eventually get to buy a couple of sweatshirts for my family. My boy wore his Ohio State T-shirt with some pride. Until he too, at last, grew out of it. Life comes full circle.

When I eventually visited the immense OSU campus with its 50,000 students, I was tickled to see that the mascot for the local American Football League team, The Buckeyes, was none other than a nut called Brutus! Yes, a nut from the Buckeye tree, native to Ohio. I just had to get one. And on the last curtain call at the Southern Theatre in Columbus, I held up my little nut-in-human-form mascot and got the biggest cheer of the entire, year-long, run. I'm not sure how Cyril will ever get over being upstaged by a small, brown, stuffed nut. Then, to everyone's amazement, we danced to the Cameo tune *Candy*, in beautiful, harmonious, line-dancing style. What a brilliantly irreverent and celebratory way to end the theatrical run of our African *Julius Caesar*. I sincerely hope that William Shakespeare would have been pleased.

We were given the greatest send-off at the end of our time in Ohio, when Mayor Coleman welcomed us to the Lincoln Theatre in downtown Columbus, for an African dance and music reception. The Lincoln is a beautifully and colourfully refurbished old proscenium-arch theatre. We all lamented that the RSC couldn't financially afford to have us play there, even for a few nights. Such a pity. Great food and a wonderful concert awaited us. A group of 18- to 25-year-olds, the Urban Strings Columbus Youth Orchestra, played skilfully. Coupled with their African dancers and drummers, we felt we were being shown the best of black excellence that the United States had to offer. Mayor Coleman moved us with his story of how this African American community had survived being evicted from their central Columbus homes early in the twentieth century. A racist town council decision to cut the black community off from the main town by building a major highway that separated them from the white community, was cynically executed. But now, fifty years later, they had succeeded in regenerating this rundown neighbourhood which had, inevitably, succumbed to the consequences of urban degeneration: negligence and crime.

That heartfelt, Columbus welcome was immensely important to us all in completing our journey – a ground-breaking, historical journey with Shakespeare's African Play, *Julius Caesar.*

* * *

I've had occasion to change my views on many things in my life, but never so frequently as during this eye-opening cultural exchange. An exchange because, as I've made clear, we, the cast, may all have shared the same skin colour but we had travelled along very different routes to get to this stage. Our personalities were, as with any large group of people, varied and complex. And yet, it is an undeniable fact that we became a kind of tribe. A theatrical army that took each city we entered to perform our play by storm. If we could harness the energy and positivity that was generated by our whole run and disseminate even a part of that to the black youth of the United Kingdom, we'd achieve in a decade what seems now to be a long struggle. The long struggle to encourage black youth to feel that they belong here in Europe. That they have vital roles to fill and a hand in their own destinies.

Playing Brutus has taught me one major thing. That we will all be faced with a moment of *discrimens* – that instant of perilous and excruciating tension when the achievements of an entire lifetime might hang in the balance. In that moment, it is imperative that we choose to be positive and act. To take a stand in our political life, a decisive reaching out for our academic or artistic destiny – a chance on trust in our intimate relations. We are all, of whatever origin, asked almost daily to decide who we are: passive drones, or active citizens. And while I disagree strongly with Brutus' methods in achieving his goals, I will always admire his courage in acting in the first place.

* * *

FIGURE 7 *The cast and crew of* Julius Caesar *at the Brooklyn Academy of Music,* April 2013.
(Photo credit: Cyril Nri)

And so, it was suddenly over. This marathon journey that had started with feelings of excitement and had gone through the darkest times that theatre productions can throw up, had culminated in our time in Ohio when I couldn't have felt more purposeful and theatre to be more relevant. Unrepeatable, like all theatre experiences, but this one was just that little bit special. The brilliant concept, the Mandela and Nyerere connections, the amazing cast, the countries and nations visited, all ensured that my learning curve rose steeply all the way through this eventful voyage.

BIBLIOGRAPHY

Primary sources

Basset, Kate. Review: 'Julius Caesar Stratford-upon-Avon . . .', *The Independent*, 9 June 2012.

Brook, Peter. *The Empty Space*. London: Penguin Modern Classics, 1968.

Capra, Fritjof. *The Tao of Physics*. Colorado: Shambhala Publications, 1975.

Carroll, Lewis. *Jabberwocky*. 1871. In *The Random House Book of Poetry for Children*. London: Random House, 1983.

Crystal, David. *The Stories of English*. London: Profile Books Ltd, 2011.

Dromgoole, Dominic. *Hamlet: Globe to Globe*. Edinburgh: Canongate Books Ltd, 2017.

Fisher, Gillian. 'Julius Caesar Review', *Afridiziak Theatre News* (http://www.afridiziak.com), 21 August 2012.

Grotowski, Jerzy. *Towards A Poor Theatre*. New York: Routledge, 1968.

Holland, Tom. *Rubicon*. England: Little, Brown and Company, 2003.

Lewis, C. S. *The Lion, the Witch and the Wardrobe*. London: Geoffrey Bles, 1950.

Mandela, Nelson. 'Speech'. 17 October 1997. Available from http://www.juliusnyerere.org/resources/view/speech_by_president_nelson_mandela_at_a_banquet_in_honour_of_julius_nyerere

Momma, Haruko and Michael Matto. *A Companion to the History of the English Language*. Chichester, West Sussex: Wiley-Blackwell, 2008.

Mugglestone, Lynda. *Talking Proper: The Rise of Accent as Social Symbol*. Oxford: Oxford University Press, 2003.

Mwenegoha, H. A. K. *Mwalimu Julius Kambarage Nyerere: A Bio-bibliography*. Foundation Books, Cambridge University Press, 1976.

Nyerere, Julius K. *The Arusha Declaration*. Dar es Salaam, 1967.

Plutarch. 'The Life of Brutus'. *Parallel Lives*. Available from http://penelope.uchicago.edu/Thayer/e/roman/texts/plutarch/lives/brutus*.html (accessed 1 September 2017).

Shapiro, James. *1599: A Year in the Life of William Shakespeare*. London: Faber and Faber, 2005.

Shapiro, James. *1606 – Shakespeare and The Year of Lear*. London: Faber and Faber, 2015.

Stanislavski, Konstantin. *My Life in Art*. United States: Little, Brown and Company, 1924.

Stanislavski, Konstantin. *An Actor Prepares*. London: Geoffrey Bles, 1937.

Stanislavski, Konstantin. *Building a Character*. London: Max Reinhardt Ltd, 1950.

Thornton, Dora and Jonathan Bate. *Shakespeare: Staging The World*. London: The British Museum Press, 2012.

Wilson, Richard. *Shakespeare: Julius Caesar. Penguin Critical Studies*. London. Penguin Books Ltd, 1992.

Productions

Holman, David. *Solomon and the Big Cat*. Prod. The Young Vic Theatre. Dir. David Thacker. 1988. (Young Vic, London)

Kwei-Armah, Kwame. *Elmina's Kitchen*. Prod. National Theatre. Dir. Angus Jackson. Design: David Williams. May 2003. (Cottesloe Theatre NT, London)

Shakespeare, William. *A Midsummer Night's Dream*. Prod. RSC. Dir. Peter Brook. Design: Sally Jacobs. 1970. (Royal Shakespeare Theatre, Stratford-upon-Avon and world tour)

Shakespeare, William. *Hamlet*. Prod. Almeida Theatre, London. Dir. Jonathan Kent. 1995. (Hackney Empire, London; Belasco Theatre, NYC)

Shakespeare, William. *Love's Labour's Lost*. Prod. RSC. Dir. Terry Hands. Design: Timothy O'Brien. 1990. (Royal Shakespeare Theatre, Stratford-upon-Avon)

Shakespeare, William. *The Tempest*. Prod. Cheek by Jowl. Dir. Declan Donnellan. Design: Nick Ormerod. August 1988. (Villa Communale, Taormina, Italy and world tour)

Sophocles. *Philoctetes*. Trans. Kenneth McLeish. Prod. Cheek by Jowl. Design: Nick Ormerod. September 1988. (Brewhouse Theatre, Taunton, UK and world tour)

The Urban Strings Columbus Youth Orchestra (urbanstrings.squarespace.com)

Shakespearean plays

Hamlet. Edited by Ann Thompson and Neil Taylor. London: Arden Shakespeare, 2006.

Julius Caesar. Edited by David Daniell. London: Arden Shakespeare, 1998.

The Merchant of Venice. Edited by John Drakakis. London: Arden Shakespeare, 2010.

Romeo and Juliet. Edited by René Weis. London: Arden Shakespeare, 2012.

Titus Andronicus. Edited by Jonathan Bate. London: Arden Shakespeare, 1994.

The Sonnets. Edited by Katherine Duncan-Jones. London: Arden Shakespeare, 1997.

Twelfth Night. Edited by Keir Elam. London: Arden Shakespeare, 2008.

Television productions

Elmina's Kitchen. Prod. BBC Four. Screenplay: Kwame Kwei-Armah. Dir. Angus Jackson. 2005. (NT Production)

Julius Caesar. William Shakespeare. Prod. BBC Four/Illuminations. Dir. Gregory Doran. 2012. (UK: BBC Four)

My Shakespeare. Prod. Channel 4. Dir. Michael Waldman. 2004. (UK/US: Channel 4 and PBS)

Shakespeare Unlocked: Julius Caesar. Prod. BBC Two, BBC Education
    Department, 2012. (UK: BBC Two) Available from http://www.bbc.co.uk/
    programmes/articles/dNP8Jwc6xc3F1hkLQfyMq5/julius-caesar (accessed 1
    September 2017).
Will Britain ever have a Black Prime Minister? Prod. BBC Two. Dir. Steve
    Grandison. 2016. (UK: BBC Two)

Translations of *Julius Caesar*

Baloyi, S. J. *Julius Caesar*. Sasavona/Swiss Mission in SA, 1957; revised version by
    Charlotte Nkondo published in 1973, reprinted by Sasavona, 1993 (Tsonga).
Mdledle, B. B. *uJulius Caesar*. A.P.B., 1957 (Xhosa).
Nemudzivadi, H. M. *Makhaulambilu a Julius Caesar*. Date and publisher unknown
    (Tshivenda).
Phatudi, N. C. *Julease Sisare*. Unieboekwinkel, 1960 (Northern Sotho).
Plaatje, Sol T. *Dintshontsho tsa bo-Julius Kesara*. Wits University, 1937 (Setswana).

ABOUT THE AUTHOR

Paterson Joseph is a British actor who has performed with the Royal Shakespeare Company and the National Theatre, among many other institutions. He has worked extensively in television and film. Joseph trained at the London Academy of Music and Dramatic Art. His theatre credits include: *Julius Caesar, Troilus and Cressida, The Last Days of Don Juan, Love's Labour's Lost, King Lear* and Ibsen's *The Pretenders* for the RSC; *Whale, The Emperor Jones, Saint Joan, Elmina's Kitchen* and *The Recruiting Officer* for the NT; *Blues for Mr Charlie, Les Blancs* and *Othello* for the Royal Exchange, Manchester; *A Doll's House* for Shared Experience; *Hamlet* for the Almeida; and *Henry IV Parts I and II* for English Touring Theatre. In 2015, he premiered his one-man play *Sancho: An Act of Remembrance* on tour in the US. Joseph's television appearances include roles in *Peep Show, Law and Order UK, Survivors, Green Wing* and *Rellik*. He has performed in several radio plays for BBC Radio 4, and appeared in films including *In the Name of the Father, The Beach* and *Aeon Flux*. Joseph is currently filming a new series of *Timeless* for NBC and will be giving *Sancho* its London premiere in June 2018.